BEHAVIOR, BIAS, AND HANDICAPS

OBSERVATIONS IN EDUCATION

Ray C. Rist, series editor

Matters of education remain an enduring debate in American society. Whether the debates focus on underlying philosophical assumptions, policy decisions, or the consequences of programs, education is one area where opinions abound and where there is little hesitance to express them. The books in this series, individually and collectively, assume the challenge of careful reflection about this most controversial of social issues. To observe American education—be it philosophical, empirical, or policy-oriented observation—is the contribution of this series. Each book probes a particular aspect of education, clarifies the questions, and works through the implications of the answers.

BEHAVIOR, BIAS, AND HANDICAPS

Labeling The Emotionally Disturbed Child

JUDY W. KUGELMASS

Transaction Books
New Brunswick (U.S.A.) and Oxford (U.K.)

Library of Congress Catalog Number: 86-30524
ISBN: 0-88738-114-6
Printed in the United States of America

Library of Congress Cataloging in Publication Data

Kugelmass, Judy W.
  Behavior, bias, and handicaps.

  Bibliography: p.
  Includes index.
  1. Mentally ill children—Education—United States.
2. Mentally ill children—United States—Identification.
3. Deviant behavior—Labeling theory.   4. Discrimination
in education—United States.   I. Title.
LC4181.K84   1987   371.94   86-30524
ISBN 0-88738-114-6

Contents

In Memory of
Marion Kugelmass

Acknowledgments

The children who attended the Medgar Evers School—in particular, the boys of the Education Center—are largely responsible for this study. In spite of the expectation that they were unwilling or unable to behave like "normal" children, the joy, warmth, and curiosity of childhood survived. Although I did not get to meet as many of their mothers as I would have liked, I want to extend my gratitude to those I met and interviewed. The struggle of single mothers in Lakeside and throughout our society needs to be acknowledged. Most are raising healthy children in spite of economic and social barriers.

I would also like to thank the many teachers who invited me into their classrooms, the principals who welcomed me into their schools, school district personnel, and members of the community who shared their perspectives with me.

To Bob Bogdan, I would like to extend my deepest appreciation both for the assistance and guidance offered throughout this study and for his making research come alive. I also wish to acknowledge Ray Rist for facilitating the publication of this book. The ideas generated by his work and that of Peter Knoblock and Steve Apter are reflected here.

I'd like to thank my friends Arlene Fingeret and Susan Foster and my children Eve and Noam for their support and encouragement. Finally, to my greatest critic, editor, proofreader, friend, and husband, Harold: thanks for putting up with the years of struggle this work represents.

1

A Historic Perspective

P.L. 94–142 and the Educational System

In 1975, the federal government attempted through the legislative process to bring about a significant change in the American educational system. As with the Civil Rights Act of 1964, the Education for All Handicapped Children Act (P.L. 94–142) was an effort to fundamentally redress an inequality in the education of children. In the case of handicapped children, a number of court decisions had established that the rights of handicapped children were being violated in that these children were being denied educations and due process protections (e.g., *Pennsylvania Association for Retarded Children* v. *Commonwealth of Pennsylvania*; *Mills* v. *Board of Education of the District of Columbia*; *Maryland* v. *Association for Retarded Children* v. *State of Maryland*). P.L. 94–142 required that all handicapped children between the ages of three and twenty–one, regardless of the severity of their handicapping condition, receive a "free, appropriate education in the least restrictive environment."

During the 1980–81 school year, nearly 3.9 million children received special education under P.L. 94–142. Approximately 300,000 of these children between the ages of five and seventeen had been identified as being handicapped as a consequence of an emotional disturbance (U.S. General Accounting Office, 1981). As handicapped children, such students became eligible under the Education for All Handicapped Children Act to receive special education and its related services (transportation; speech, occupational, and physical therapy and psychological counseling) at no cost to their families. Although prior legislation (Section 504 of the Rehabilitation Act of 1973) had mandated that all recipients of federal funds provide equal access to education for all students, regardless of their handicapping conditions, P.L. 94–142 allocated funds and provided regulations for this specific purpose.

Many of the children labeled as emotionally disturbed had not benefited from the traditional teaching methods followed in most public schools. An appropriate education for these children might have meant approaching

1

them through a variety of teaching styles, tapping their sensory and affective processes rather than, or in addition to their linguistic processes. Instructional objectives needed to be developed that were geared toward meeting the child's specific cognitive and affective needs. The challenges these children presented offered the educational system an opportunity to expand its repertoire of teaching strategies and its methods of grouping children. Now that handicapped children were included in public schools, a group of children of similar chronological age within a given school could no longer be assumed to represent a homogeneous group nor would the same teaching approach be appropriate for every child.

The majority of school districts throughout the United States have not, however, provided educational programs for children identified as emotionally disturbed within their regular educational system. Instead, an educational system parallel to the regular education system has been developed. The majority of these special education systems provide educational programs for children labeled as emotionally disturbed in classrooms segregated from their typical peers (Grosenick & Huntze, 1980; U.S. General Accounting Office, 1981). "Mainstreaming," i.e. including the handicapped child in a regular classroom with typical peers, is not the norm in spite of the fact that research has not demonstrated significant educational or social benefits for mildly or moderately handicapped children placed in special education classrooms (Dunn, 1968; Knoblock, 1983; Vacc, 1972) and that P.L. 94-142 directs that children be educated in the "least restrictive environment." Educational programs for deviant children have been developed that have not demanded significant alterations in the form or content of the regular educational system.

Emotional Disturbance in Children: A Historical Overview

The separation of deviant children from their peers is not a recent invention of special education. The American education system has historically excluded and/or segregated children who were perceived as abnormal. Tracing the treatment of children during the nineteenth and twentieth centuries who had been thought of as emotionally disturbed illustrates the precedents for today's programs.

It is important to remember that prior to the eighteenth century, behaviors which today would be defined as deviant, delinquent or disturbed, were then thought of as common and conventional.

As late as the 17th century, children engaged in behaviors that would today be defined as delinquency: most learned and used obscene language regularly, many freely engaged in a variety of sexual activities, some drank regularly in taverns. (Conrad & Schneider, 1980, p. 147)

Children during that period who behaved in ways that were considered bizarre were believed to be under the influence of demonic possession. Treatment for these children often took the form of cruel punishment, medical treatments such as bleedings, or lifetime incarceration in "lunatic asylums." It was not until after the French Revolution that humane treatment for markedly deviant individuals was attempted. Phillipe Pinel, a French physician, demonstrated that chronic mental patients who had been chained and brutalized for years in the Bicetre Hospital in Paris could show dramatic improvement in their behavior when treated with kindness and respect. However, no distinction was made between the treatment of adults and children, or between individuals who would today be identified as mentally retarded rather than emotionally disturbed.

One of the first accounts of the treatment of a severely disturbed child came from Jean Marc Gaspard Itard (1894), a student of Pinel. In *The Wild Boy of Aveyron*, Itard demonstrated how social and emotional isolation could result in behaviors that many believed to be evidence of incurable "idiocy." Victor, the boy Itard found running wild in the woods of Aveyron in 1799, responded to teaching strategies that incorporated a multisensory approach applied systematically to elicit specific responses (Knoblock, 1983) that would be reinforced both by the stimulation they provided and by Itard's enthusiasm and love.

Unfortunately, neither Pinel's nor Itard's approach took hold in the United States during the nineteenth century. Instead, deviant behaviors began to be thought of as social problems.

> The Jacksonian era, beginning in the 1820's, contrasted to earlier times by focusing on remedial efforts based on the need for order in society. Social and environmental interventions were designed and implemented both to correct deviant behaviors and to create social institutions beyond the family that could encourage greater social stability. (Knoblock, 1983, p. 7)

These institutions included mental hospitals, almshouses for the poor, and penitentiaries for adults and juveniles. Their aim was the rehabilitation of their charges. The treatment offered was segregation from society, isolation, and harsh discipline, along with the highly structured routines of the institutions. Physicians maintained leadership of these institutions and were strong advocates of the segregation of their inmates from the rest of society. The deviant behaviors of their patients were indeed a social problem, but the roots of these disorders were believed to lie not within society, but within the individual's biophysical nature.

As the nineteenth century progressed, compulsory education laws were put into effect throughout the United States. Increased urbanization and industrialization swelled the numbers of working-class and immigrant children in northeastern cities. They were largely perceived as deficient in both their intellectual and social skills. No attempts were made to alter the methods of instruction to fit these children's lifestyles or to recognize the positive attributes such children may have brought to school. Rather, the practices employed by school systems were geared at keeping working-class children "alert, obedient, and so thoroughly attuned to discipline through group sanctions that a minimum of policing would assure the preservation of social order"(Katz, 1971, p. 11).

An interesting parallel can be drawn between the ways in which the educational system responded to the compulsory education laws enacted between 1852 and 1919 and the ways in which today's system has responded to P.L. 94–142. In each instance, children whose behaviors were perceived as deviant were thrust upon the system. Public policy demanded that these children be educated, and that the schools act as a socializing force. At the turn of the century, large numbers of immigrant and working-class children entered into school systems that operated under sets of expectations regarding both the role of the teacher and the behavior of students. Then, as now, in schools that included handicapped children, a mismatch occurred between the children's needs and expectations and those of their teachers. At the turn of the century, the system responded not by altering its assumptions, but rather by developing a "sorting-out process" for students:

> A sorting-out process gradually evolved, and ungraded classes were begun for children who did not fit into regular classrooms. These included children who were below average intellectually or functionally as well as "incorrigible" and non-English-speaking children. Thus, two early developments have persisted to the present. First, school populations are sorted out and labeled as being deviant or in need of special help (groups often composed primarily of poor and minority group children). Second, reliance on special classes as the major programming intervention remains very much in effect today. (Knoblock, 1983, p. 18)

The sorting, labeling and segregation of deviant children in public schools gained continued legitimacy with the Mental Hygiene movement, which began in 1909. Clifford Beers, considered the founder of this movement, had himself been institutionalized in a "mental hospital." In his autobiography, *A Mind That Found Itself* (1908), he recalled his experiences and the emotional turmoil of his life. He and his colleagues hoped to prevent mental disorders and institutionalization by providing early detection and prevention programs through child guidance clinics and mental hygiene programs in the schools. These programs called on physicians to advise teachers "in the treatment and training of children":

> Particularly this is so in the cases of nervous disturbances, as we all know, city children, because of the conditions of urban life, are particularly liable. Nervous troubles frequently beset the child and prevent his getting the full advantage of education, and if unchecked, or if aggravated by school work, have serious consequences in adult life. (Berkowitz & Rothman, 1967, p. 9)

However well-intentioned, the Mental Hygiene Movement did not significantly alter what was going on inside the New York City public schools. The medical model it adopted, although recognizing that the causes of the child's "nervous condition" might lie within his or her interactions with various environments, focused its interventions on the child. A "nervous disturbance" was the symptom of a problem that belonged to the child who needed to be treated. These "treatments" were carried out in "probationary" schools that segregated the deviant child from his peers.

Certainly the advances in the study of human psychology that were in the foreground of the early twentieth century gave added impetus to the Mental Hygiene Movement. William Healy and his colleagues in Chicago had begun a systematic study of repeated juvenile offenders. Alfred Binet had introduced his intelligence scale, which would measure children's intellectual functioning, predict their school performance, and provide a tool for sorting children accordingly. Sigmund Freud and his followers had begun writing extensively on both infantile sexuality and human intrapsychic development. Each of these influenced and encouraged the development of the Mental Hygiene movement. The decision to remove problem children from the public schools was not, however, the result of these influences alone.

The school system was threatened by the large numbers of lower-class and immigrant children it was charged with educating. The underlying assumption of the school system was that its mission was to instill conformity, neatness, and dependence in its students while teaching them basic skills (Katz, 1971). Faced with thousands of nonconforming, dirty, and defiant children, the system had two clear choices. It could modify its expectations and assumptions and develop educational practices that would accommodate the lifestyles of its students, or it could become more deeply committed to its mission and develop a more efficient system for carrying out its goals. Because the conceptual orientation of the Mental Hygiene Movement was wedded to the medical model of understanding deviant behavior, and because the school system held fast to its convictions, the Mental Hygiene Movement did not bring radical change to the school system. Rather, it helped to support the shared understandings among school personnel regarding what they believed to be normal childhood behavior, and provided a "scientifically" based treatment for those children who did not conform to this understanding.

Under the guidance of the Mental Hygiene Movement, special schools were established in New York City to deal with deviant children. As is the case with children who have been labeled "emotionally disturbed" in public schools today, the students sent to these schools were primarily discipline problems (Grosenick & Huntze, 1980). Most came from lower-class families, and all were boys. These schools continued to operate throughout this century and, in 1946, were designated as "600" schools. The "600" school concept gradually expanded to include residential settings, as well as day schools, for both girls and boys.

In 1965, the New York City school system replaced the "600" numbers assigned to schools serving problem children with names and random numbers, in the hope of reducing the stigma that had become attached to the children attending those schools. The "600" schools had become places where the "bad kids," now labeled "emotionally disturbed," were sent. These children were primarily Blacks from low socioeconomic backgrounds. In 1978, as a consequence of the segregated nature of these schools, the United States District Court found that the New York City school system had been violating the rights of large numbers of its Black students by placing them in "600" schools. The court's decree read as follows: "To the extent that students were referred to largely racially segregated schools, it was denial of equal educational opportunity in violation of Title VI" (*Lora* v. *The Board of Education of the City of New York, 1978*).

The identification of low-income Black children as "disturbed," and their placement in segregated programs illustrate what has been described by many authors as the sociopolitical functions of the mental health and/ or educational systems (Conrad & Schneider, 1980; Hurley, 1966; Katz, 1971; Rhodes, 1970, 1972; Rhodes & Gibbins, 1972; Ryan, 1971; Scheff, 1966, 1974; Szasz, 1966, 1974). Rhodes' (1972) analysis of this function is particularly relevant in understanding both the evolution of the Mental Hygiene Movement in New York City and the data presented in this study. He postulates that when individuals in relative positions of power are confronted by behaviors that threaten their psycho-social equilibrium, a "threat–recoil cycle" is activated.

> Such cycles can develop a velocity that creates upset and agitation across the nation and involves major segments of the population in their turbulence. (Rhodes, 1972, p. 10)

Although this process is seen as a constant part of community life, which is called upon to protect the community from both physical and psychological threats, there are periods when the stress cycle becomes profound.

Conceptual Models for Understanding Emotional Disturbance in Children

The interventions that were developed to deal with deviant children in New York City were based upon a shared understanding on the part of professionals regarding the meaning of these children's behavior. This understanding rests upon a conceptual model that defines deviant behavior as evidence of an illness within the child. This, in turn, influenced the kinds of interventions that were established. This process is not unique to New York but has been demonstrated in the literature to have operated elsewhere in programs designed to serve children who are considered to be emotionally disturbed (Rhodes & Tracy, Vols. I & II, 1977).

> In an intervention, the conceptual framework directs and channels the action, by providing an analysis of the nature of the problem which dictates the intervention, and by suggesting the outcomes toward which the intervention is directed. (Rhodes & Tracey, 1973, Vol. II, p. 23)

Both the Mental Hygiene Movement and the programs for children identified as emotionally disturbed described in this study were based upon a medical model of explaining deviant behavior in children. Although the conditions of urban life had been recognized, in each case, as playing a part in the child's condition, the remedy took the form of offering treatment to the child. Neither program attempted interventions that treated aspects of the child's life in the real world. Certainly, a school based mental health program could not take on the task of altering the economic structure of our society or ending racism. But, once the conditions of a troubled child's life are recognized as being responsible for his or her behavior, interventions must include improving these conditions. Helping a young, single mother to budget her welfare allotment while giving her support, parenting skills, nutrition information, prevocational training, and recreational opportunities are, for example, some of the services programs for disturbed children from low-income, single–parent families should include. Interventions that operate from the medical model perspective generally will not include these kinds of services. Instead, the child is the focus of the intervention. The child is perceived as being "sick" and therefore is the person in need of treatment.

This perspective follows primarily from a psychodynamic understanding of abnormal behavior. Aggressive and antisocial behaviors are seen as evidence of inadequate ego development and/or deficiencies in superego controls. These are thought to have come about because of inadequate socialization, which left the child at the mercy of his unrestrained impulses (Aichorn, 1935; Redl & Wineman, 1957). Based on Freudian, psychoanalytic conceptualizations, this model focuses its attention on the child's intrapsychic life and development. This development is perceived as one which normally proceeds along a biologically determined path, following stages which correspond to the child's physiological development. Movement from one stage to another involves the successful resolution of conflicts which are inherent to each stage. Considered of greatest significance in developing a healthy psyche for males is the resolution of the Oedipus conflict. This requires that the boy sublimate his desire for sexual intercourse with his mother by assimilating the values, beliefs and personality of his father. In the attainment of this identification with his father, the boy develops his super-ego, or conscience, and an appropriate sexual identity. This aspect of a child's socialization is seen as vital for normal psychological development.

Although there have been many modifications in psychoanalytic theory to include socialization experiences in other cultures (Erikson, 1963), the two-parent family predominates as the family structure that is thought to be essential for normal, healthy psychological adjustment. Data derived from the 1980 U.S. Census illustrate, however, that among Whites, approximately 12 percent of all families with children under eighteen years of age live in families headed by females. Among Blacks who responded to census questionnaires, approximately 33 percent reported that single females were the heads of households. It is estimated that the majority of Black children (55%) are today born to unmarried, often teenage mothers (Andersen, 1984). Following an orthodox psychoanalytic perspective, one would view the children in these nearly five million families to be at serious risk for emotional disturbance, not because of the poverty that is rampant among them and the stresses that accompany poverty, but because of children's unresolved Oedipal conflicts.

Although those following a psychoanalytic perspective would argue that its concepts are based on a scientific understanding of human behavior, it is clear that a good many of its conceptualizations are based on culturally biased beliefs. As Jean Baker-Miller (1982), a psychoanalytically trained psychiatrist, points out, the belief in the two-parent family is one of this perspective's strongest biases:

> Long tradition tends to foster the belief that a family headed by a woman cannot be an adequate family; it is a "broken family." Further, as Ladner pointed out in a study of a Black community, the professional absorbs the

values of the dominant culture; and the culture tends to judge by the standards of the dominant middle-class. (p. 351)

Recent investigations into the effects of divorce on children point out
that emotional disturbance need not be the inevitable outcome for children raised in single–parent families (Guidubaldi & Perry, 1984; Waller-
stein, 1984). Understanding the dynamics underlying the problems
confronting children raised in single parent families involves an exploration into many aspects of a given child's life. These include not only child
variables such as age, sex, physical health, and intellectual and developmental status, but also the relationships and interactions the child may
experience both within the family system and within the community, including the school. The economic hardships facing the single parent family
combine with inadequate day care, few formal community supports, and
social networks that may further promote family dysfunction. Such
stressed family environments get expressed in inadequate parenting which,
in turn, may be reflected in children's behavior. In spite of this, programs
for troubled children, such as the one described in this book, often do not
offer the low-income, single mother the kinds of supports that might relieve
this stress.

Instead, following a psychoanalytic understanding of behavior, the problems exhibited by children from such families are often explained as psychiatric symptoms. Thus, as Szasz (1966) has pointed out, "mental illness"
is made into the cause of the "problems of living" experienced by these
children, rather than seen as its result. Rule-breaking behavior becomes
understood in terms of psychiatric symptoms (Scheff, 1966). This definition of behavior is particularly questionable when applied to children who
are in the process of learning the rules of social behavior. Their behavior is
often transitory and related to their developmental status. Children are
also in the position of interacting with those in authority who hold different tolerances and/or attach different meanings to similar behaviors.

For example, it has been found that when teachers are asked to identify
children with behavior problems, boys are selected more often than girls
(Werry & Quay, 1971). However, when parents are asked, there are no
significant differences between the numbers of boys and girls identified
(Ross, 1980). This can be understood in terms of the different tolerances
held by parents and teachers, as well as the demands placed on children in
both settings, with school perhaps being a more aversive situation for boys
than for girls. Clearly, looking only at the child's overt behavior in school
does not present a complete understanding of the problems facing this
child.

The discrepancies that exist between teachers' and parents' understandings of deviant behavior can be understood when the identification of

children as mentally ill or emotionally disturbed is approached from the perspective of "labeling" theory (Becker, 1963; Kitsuse, 1964; Rist & Harrell, 1982; Rubington & Weinberg, 1973; Scheff, 1966, 1974; Szasz, 1966). According to the labeling perspective, there is no absolute or clear consensus regarding which behaviors represent a norm violation, particularly in a heterogeneous society. Behaviors that may be considered appropriate in one setting may be perceived as deviant in another. Middle-class children may, in fact, have less difficulty in conforming to the behavioral expectations of school than lower-class children, not because they are never disobedient, aggressive, or overtly defiant, but rather because they have been exposed to more of a variety of social situations and have learned a fact of life essential for survival in a complex and highly heterogeneous society: different social situations demand different behaviors, and different people have different expectations and tolerances.

When professionals who operate from a medical model perspective label children who exhibit problem behaviors at school as emotionally disturbed, the child and his or her family are most often seen as responsible for the child's problem. The focus of exploration into the child's problems in school may then shift away from the school environment itself, its teachers, its curriculum, its overall culture. It is the child that is "sick." The notion that deviant behavior is a symptom of an illness also carries with it the connotation that other children may become contaminated. This line of reasoning may, in fact, be responsible for the fact that children labeled as emotionally disturbed are often quarantined in groups, i.e., in classrooms segregated from "typical" students.

Certainly, children cannot be permitted to behave in ways that threaten the physical safety of others or that interfere with other students' education. However, despite the fact that some children identified as emotionally disturbed are indeed very angry, most present no danger to other children or their teachers. This is particularly true of young children (5–11 years old), such as those described in this book. Most are kids who have never what teachers expect. When these children are faced with teachers who are not afraid to confront them directly and who are willing to offer support, appropriate skill training, and nurturing, disruptive children become functional members of classrooms. Teachers who understand children's behavior within the context of the community and families of which they are a part, do not perceive an acting out, even aggressive child as a threat. Instead, the child is seen as having the same needs as other children but lacking a knowledge of how to behave in the social environment of a school.

The notion that children who have been identified as emotionally disturbed have not learned appropriate behaviors, or, conversely, that they have learned inappropriate behaviors, is the basic premise of a behavioristic conceptualization. Behaviorists prefer the term "behavior disorder" to that of "emotional disturbance." From this perspective, deviant or disordered behavior are considered to have been learned. Like any other behaviors, these have been elicited and maintained by environmental reinforcements and can be modified by a sequenced program of rewards and punishments. Therefore, behavior modification programs aim at shaping the child's behavior to conform to the expectations, demands, and rules of the school.

Defining the deviant child as having a "behavior disorder" rather than an "emotional disturbance" is believed to be a more objective description. Looking at overt behavior rather than hypothesizing about unseen psychodynamic processes that may be motivating the child is believed to be a more empirically based and therefore more "scientific" conceptualization. Judging a behavior as inappropriate is not, however, an objective decision. Rather, as Buckholdt and Gubrium (1979) demonstrated in their study of a residential school for children labeled as emotionally disturbed, a good deal of subjective judgment is used in deciding which behaviors are disordered and which are appropriate. It is not the behavior, but rather the meaning attached to it by a particular teacher, that determines whether or not it will be targeted for modification.

When a child is identified as either "emotionally disturbed" or "behaviorally disordered," the focus of attention is placed on that child. The behavior disorder is still conceived of as something the child *has*, rather than something he or she *does*, in a given situation. Mash and Terdal (1981), two behavioral psychologists, believe that many of the problems faced in the identification of children either as behaviorally disordered or emotionally disturbed are the result of a lack of conceptual and methodological clarity, both in the understanding of childhood disorders and in the methods used for assessment. They propose an approach that looks not only at overt behaviors, as is frequently done by the use of behavioral checklists (Cone & Hawkins, 1977), but also at the "interacting social systems" in which the child is involved, as well as at the child's cognitive and affective styles.

One child's grabbing a toy away from another is, for example, not necessarily a negative interaction. In fact, it may demonstrate positive development for a given child, within a given peer group. A child's behavior must first of all be understood within the context of his or her peer group (Foster & Richey, 1979). Children often attach different meanings to the behavior of their peers than do adults. Their acceptance of each other is often based on nonbehavioral characteristics, such as physical attractiveness, body type, reputation, and the special skills and abilities one might have. Without knowledge of a child's value system, which may, in part, reflect his or her ethnic subculture, adults may misjudge a child's behavior.

Virginia Axline (1969), a highly renowned child psychotherapist, illustrated how she misinterpreted a child's behavior by failing to understand it from the child's perspective. After many weeks of seeing a young Black child for play therapy, she saw no progress in the treatment nor any evidence that he was relating to her in any way. Week after week, this boy would sit at a table with his feet up on it, tilting his chair back, arms folded, with an impassive expression on his face. Ms. Axline began to feel that perhaps this child's "resistance" was too strong to be overcome by traditional, nondirective play therapy techniques. When, finally, the boy turned to her and said, "Know what I've been playing? I've been playing White Man!" Ms. Axline realized she had been interpreting his behavior from within the context of her own experience.

Deviance in children has not been studied to the same extent as it has in adults (Des Jarlais, 1977). Children are in the process of learning the rules of society. This socialization process presupposes a certain amount of rule violation because the child is only a partially socialized being. The consequences for rule breaking are therefore different for children than for adults. Every culture makes allowances for certain behaviors in its children at different stages of their development. This permissiveness is relative to the values a culture wishes to transmit through the socialization process.

In a heterogeneous society such as ours, children are socialized in many different ways. Our schools, however, evaluate children's behavior from a more narrow perspective (Mercer, 1973). Because of this, the rule-breaking behavior of minority children may often be interpreted as symptomatic of an emotional disturbance. This is clearly the case in the city of Lakeside, where 80 percent of all children identified as "severely emotionally disturbed" are Black and male. On a national level as well, Black children are generally overrepresented in public school programs for the emotionally disturbed (U.S. General Accounting Office, 1981).

Literature focusing on the interaction between the Black child and the school system demonstrates that a child enters the school not as a "blank slate" (tabula rasa), but as a social being who has interacted with his environment and the significant individuals in it (Henry, 1971; Ogbu, 1974; Riessman, 1962; Rist, 1970, 1973; Silverstein & Krate, 1975). It is through this interaction, or socialization process, that he or she has learned to internalize the patterns of behavior and the value system they represent. The value system or culture that has nurtured the child until this point is the one to which he or she owes an emotional and intellectual allegiance. A conflict occurs when the values and expectations of the school contradict those the child has learned, or when the same behavior has different meanings to the child and those in authority.

Studies of the Bureau of Indian Affairs' schools for the Sioux Indians offer examples of this lack of fit between the schools' expectations of appropriate behavior and the meaning this same behavior has for Indian children (Erikson, 1963; Henry, 1971; Wax & Wax, 1971). Sharing and generosity are important values for the Sioux; in the past, they served an important function in the maintenance of the tribe. Early childhood training (socialization and education) incorporated these values into the child. When the Sioux child enters the American school, the expectation of the teacher will probably be that the student will take pride in his own efforts and achievements. If the child fails to respond to the teacher's questions, he or she may be viewed as "withdrawn" or "incompetent." The meaning a teacher attaches to a child's behavior is often the consequence of the teacher's socialization and education and may not reflect the reality of the child's behavior taken from the perspective of the child.

Wax and Wax (1971) elaborate on this misunderstanding:

> For in this system an individual may excel only when his excellence enhances the position of his brethren. If this achievement were to derogate them before others, then it would be incumbent on him to conceal his talents. Thus, in the schools on Pine Ridge, our staff observed classrooms where, when a teacher called upon a pupil to recite, he would become the target of jibes and jokes whispered in Lakota and unperceived by his teacher, with the result that he would stand or sit paralyzed and unable to respond; meanwhile, the teacher, being oblivious to the secret life of the classroom, would be perplexed and distressed at her inability to secure responses indicating that she had covered the day's lessons. (p. 7)

In the same way that the Sioux child's behavior has been perceived by those in authority as evidence of his pathology (i.e., it is defined as "withdrawn"), so may the Black child's behavior (i.e., it is defined as "aggressive") be used as evidence of his emotional disturbance. This illustrates a mismatch between the teacher's and the student's perception of the situation. Two related theoretical perspectives of symbolic interactionism (Blumer, 1969; Mead, 1934) and that of human ecology can be called upon for an explanation of this phenomenon.

The first of these relates to the individual's perception of the situation:

> For these theorists [i.e., symbolic interactionists], people are constantly in a process of *interpretation* and *definition* as they move from one situation to another. Some situations are familiar, such as one's home, school or workplace; others are less familiar and may be one-encounter affairs. All situations

consist of the actor, others and their actions, and physical objects. In any case, a situation has *meaning* only through people's interpretations and definitions of it. Their actions, in turn, stem from this meaning. Thus, this process of interpretation acts as the intermediary between any predisposition to act and the action itself. (Bogdan & Taylor, 1975, p. 14)

The "deviancy" or "labeling" perspective expands this theoretical framework and focuses on the act of identifying or interpreting certain behaviors as deviant and the consequence of this phenomenon.

All social groups make rules and attempt, at some times and under some circumstances, to enforce them. Social rules define situations and the kind of behavior appropriate to them, specifying some actions as "right" and forbidding others as "wrong." When a rule is enforced, the person who is supposed to have broken it may be seen as a special kind of person, one who cannot be trusted to live by the rules agreed upon by the group. He is regarded as an *outsider*. (Becker, 1963, p. 1)

Thus, children who break the social rules of school may become identified as deviant and are labeled as such. This process does not occur in the same way for all individuals, even when they behave in the same kinds of ways. The deviancy of their act is determined not only by the act, but also by the meaning the act is given by those in power. The social status of the rule breaker is seen as an important variable in determining whether or not the act is perceived as threatening and in need of sanctions.

The degree to which an act will be treated as deviant depends on who commits the act and who feels he has been harmed by it. Rules tend to be applied more to some persons than to others. Studies of juvenile delinquency make the point clearly. Boys from middle-class areas do not get as far in the legal process when they are apprehended as do boys from slum areas. (Becker, 1963, p. 13)

Ecological theory represents a second and related point of view that can further clarify the interaction between students and teachers. Wilson (1977) points out that not only do the individuals influence reality by their definition of the situation, but that the setting itself generates regularities in behavior. Therefore, the behavior of individuals must be examined in context. Human ecologists stress the importance of "fit" between an individual and his or her environment. There is a continual interaction between the two. In the case of organizations, such as schools, this interaction can be seen as a consistent pattern of behavior by its members, which allows for the continuation of the organization and the perpetuation of its pattern of operation (Rhodes & Tracy, Vol. I, 1972).

Ecological theory presents an alternative conceptual framework through which the identification of children as emotionally disturbed can be understood (Algozzine, 1976, 1977; Apter, 1982; Hobbs, 1975, 1980; Rhodes, 1970; Ross, 1980; Salzinger, Antrobus, & Glick, 1980; Swap, 1974, 1978). Apter (1982) defines emotional disturbance from an ecological perspective in the following way:

> From this outlook, emotional disturbance is not simply seen as the necessary result of intrapsychic conflict nor as the inevitable product of inappropriate social learning. Instead, according to the ecological model, disturbance resides in the interaction between a child and the critical aspects of the child's environment, that is, the child's system. More specifically, ecological theorists believe that what we know as emotional disturbance or behavior disorders actually result from discrepancies between a given child's skills and abilities and the demands or expectations of that child's environment. (p. 2)

Salzinger, Antrobus, and Glick (1980) call for a functional concept of disturbed behavior in children, that is, not a collection of symptoms residing in the child, as is presented by both psychodynamic and behavioral models of disturbance, "but rather as a set of behaviors that, with reference to different social contexts, is either rejected or accepted as appropriate and thereby normal. Disturbed behavior is largely defined by the society itself as behavior that is unacceptable in the situation in which it occurs in its present form and this is selected for modification." (p. 4)

From an ecological perspective, emotional disturbance is not a condition that resides within the child alone, but is the result of a "mismatch" that has occurred between the child and the "ecological systems" of which the child is a part. Understanding a child's behavior involves more than assessing the child's deficits and assets or developmental and pschophysiological status. The child's behavior must also be seen in the context of an "ecological network" that contains three nested systems. The first of these is the "behavior setting," i.e., the place where the disturbing behavior occurs. The "disturbingness" of the behavior is a "product of the interaction between the child and elements of the setting" (Swap, 1978, p. 187). Next, patterns of behavior across various settings must be looked at to see if the child's behavior is consistent across settings, or if it is peculiar to one environment. This must be seen within the context of the community and culture of both the child and those in authority who have defined his behavior as disturbed.

Approaching the study of the emotionally disturbed child from both a deviancy and ecological perspective allows for a more complete understanding of these children and the labeling process. Their behavior has been judged as deviant in the behavior setting of classrooms by teachers who hold a particular set of expectations regarding appropriate behavior in that setting. Assessment of these children has not traditionally included an exploration of their behavior in other settings. Rather, they are judged as deviant based on school behaviors that have violated school norms. If the form of this rule breaking corresponds to behaviors that have been defined as symptoms of disturbance, and this definition is given official approval through formal regulations and procedures, the children exhibiting these behaviors will be labeled as emotionally disturbed.

2

Labeling: An Ecological Perspective

P.L. 94–142 and the Emotionally Disturbed Child

The following definition of emotional disturbance, as written in the Education for All Handicapped Children Act of 1975 (P.L. 94–142), is based on a medical model of understanding deviant behavior. This definition does not include a consideration of the child's behavior across settings.

'Seriously emotionally disturbed' is defined as follows. The term means a condition exhibiting one or more of the following characteristics over a long period of time and to a marked degree, which adversely affects educational performance: (a) an inability to learn which cannot be explained by intellectual, sensory, or health factors; (b) an inability to build or maintain satisfactory interpersonal relationships with peers and teachers; (c) inappropriate types of behavior or feelings under normal circumstances; (d) a general pervasive mood of unhappiness or depression or (e) a tendency to develop physical symptoms or fears associated with personal or school problems. The term includes children who are schizophrenic or autistic. The term does not include children who are socially maladjusted, unless it is determined that they are seriously emotionally disturbed (Education for All Handicapped Children Act, 1975).

This definition was taken from the work of Eli M. Bower (1969). His original definition was more specific and, although resting on psychodynamic conceptualizations, included situational variables and a continuum of behavior ranging from what he considered to be mild disorders to those more severe. Originally, Bower distinguished between those children who were experiencing "problems of everyday living, growing, exploring and reality testing" (p. 27) and those with more classic psychiatric symptoms. P.L. 94–142's definition makes no such distinction.

Problems in the classification of children as emotionally disturbed extend to service delivery systems outside of education. Although psychiatric classifications such as those found in the *Diagnostic and Statistical Manual of Mental Disorders* (D.S.M. III) and in the work of the Group for the Advancement of Psychiatry and the World Health Organization have, in recent years, been reorganized to be more descriptive and to take a child's developmental status into account, these systems share the same problems as the educational system's classification of children as emotionally disturbed. Children's deviant behaviors are conceptualized as symptoms of diseases of their personality structures and hypothesized parts of their psyche (Kauffman, 1981).

The following, taken from the work of Nicholas Hobbs (1975, 1980), represents some of the major deficits shared by current classification schemes:

1. Children are placed in categories which obscure individual differences within each category.
2. There is an assumption inherent to these systems that the problem lies exclusively within the child.
3. Children are usually assigned to one category. However, the more severe a handicapping condition, the more likely there are multiple problems. Although DSM III tries to address this problem to some extent, it lacks the descriptive clarity that is necessary for gathering accurate prevalence and incidence data.
4. These systems are based on deficit models, i.e., no attention is given to a child's strengths.
5. There is a tendency for classification systems to be static and therefore not enough attention is paid to developmental and situational changes. This results in a reduced expectancy to change and invites a confirmation of the behavior expected in each category.
6. Classification systems encourage the labeling of children.
7. Children who may best be described as fitting "between" two categories are often "lost."
8. Services may be fragmented because of the divisions which occur between different service delivery systems using different classification schemes.
9. Because current classification systems do not describe anything about the needs of individual children and the services they may require, assessment for accountability and planning is hindered.

Hobbs proposes an ecologically oriented, service-based classification system. Such a system would take into account the situational, developmental, and transactional nature of the child's needs. The services needed by a particular child would be the goal of assessment, rather than the diagnosis being an end in and of itself. Implementing an ecologically oriented classification and service delivery system would mean that responsibility for the child's behavior would be shared by the other individuals with whom the child interacts. Deviant behavior would then be viewed not as symptomatic of a disease located within the child, but rather as evidence of "discordance" in the system.

> Discordance may be defined as a disparity between an individual's abilities and the demands and expectations of the environment—a "failure to match" between the child and the system. It is not the child alone or the environment alone that causes emotional disturbance. Rather it is the interaction between them that creates a discordance and disrupts the system. (Apter, 1982, p.17)

The fit between the child and the system can be improved either by altering the child's behavior and/or the environment, or by reevaluating the demands and expectations placed on the child. The latter includes redefining the child's behavior from a perspective that includes the child's way of viewing the world. This conceptualization would present basic challenges to the way our educational system historically has operated. P.L. 94–142 was developed within a conceptual framework that would not require significant alterations in the educational system in order to provide educational opportunities for students previously excluded.

Certainly, schools have had to change in order to serve handicapped children. Children who are experiencing failure in school cannot be ignored by the school once a referral is made to a school district's Committee on the Handicapped by a parent, teacher, psychologist, or any individual concerned with the child's performance in school. This committee, mandated by P.L. 94–142, consists of, *at least*, a teacher or administrator in the field of special education, a parent of a handicapped child, a psychologist, and a physician. The school district may also appoint other educators or school personnel as voting members. The committee is charged with reviewing all children brought before and determining whether or not a handicapping condition exists, as defined by state and federal regulations. Such children must be evaluated, using assessment procedures in the child's native language, within 30 days of the original referral.

The child's parents or legal guardians must be informed, in writing, of the referral and the date of any evaluation the committee recommends. The parents are then invited to attend a meeting of the committee, at which time the results of the evaluation will be discussed and recommendations made. Parents may accept or reject the committee's decisions and ask for an impartial hearing. An "Impartial Hearing Officer" from outside the school district is appointed by the state education department to serve as judge in this quasilegal hearing. If, however, the parents and committee agree, the child is labeled as having a handicapping condition (e.g., mentally retarded, emotionally disturbed, learning disabled, autistic, blind, deaf, health impaired, orthopedically impaired, speech impaired, or multiply handicapped).

The particular label applied to the child will depend upon the conformity of the child's behavior and school achievement to the criteria given in both federal and state regulations. This process is supposed to provide the means for objective decision making. However, it is clear that there is a good deal of subjective judgment involved in both the identification of and programming for children labeled as handicapped. This is particularly true in those categories of disability that relate primarily to a child's functioning in school, i.e., learning disabled (L.D.), educable mentally retarded (E.M.R.), and emotionally disturbed (E.D.). Each of these categories represents a designation of deviancy to children whose skills and/or behaviors do not match those expected in school. Most of these children can function competently outside of school and will be indistinguishable from the general population once they leave the formal educational system (Sarason & Doris, 1979).

A child can be labeled as learning disabled if a significant discrepancy exists between academic functioning and presumed "potential." The learning disabled child does not acheive academically because of a hypothesized underlying dysfunction that is often presumed to be genetic, structural, neurological, or biochemical. In most cases the organic nature of the disability cannot be medically determined but is assumed as the explanation for why this otherwise intelligent child is failing in school.

The child labeled as educable mentally retarded, on the other hand, is assumed to be a failure in school because of his limited "potential." Such children's I.Q. scores fall below the low average range and above that considered to be indicative of severe mental retardation. For a child to be labeled as mentally retarded, regardless of the degree of presumed retardation, he or she must also display deficits in adaptive behavior. This means that the child's ability to function socially does not correspond to what is expected of the average child of the same chronological age. This social maladaption is understood to be a consequence of the child's limited intelligence.

Children who are identified as emotionally disturbed as well as those labeled as learning disabled or educable mentally retarded, also display deficits in academic achievement and in social behavior, as defined by the school. However, programs for each group of children differ in their emphases on teaching academic skills. This difference can be seen as related to the meaning given to underachievement for each of these handicapping conditions. For the learning disabled child, for example, underachievement is the primary factor in his or her identification, and so becomes the focus of intervention (perceptual motor training or multisensory approaches to reading, for example). These children underachieve because they are learning disabled. Their misbehavior is understood to be the result of a lack of internal controls, the misreading of social cues, or the manifestation of anxiety states related to their failure to achieve. For the educable mentally retarded children, however, underachievement for their chronological age is expected because of their low measured I.Q.s. Misbehaviors on their part are taken as examples of deficits in adaptive behavior, which are expected in individuals of low intellectual ability. Since it is assumed they cannot think abstractly, E.M.R. children are "taught" by rote drill, programmed teaching strategies and direct instruction in activities of daily living rather than by active problem solving (Gajar, 1977; Hallahan & Kauffman, 1977; Quay & Galvin, 1970).

Emotionally disturbed children misbehave because they are emotionally disturbed. Their underachievement is believed to be a consequence of their inappropriate social behavior and/or affective disorder. Once their behavior and/or emotional disorder is resolved, it is assumed that learning will proceed normally. Programming for these children often focuses on altering their behavior and/or affective states, with less attention given to academic instruction or to the child's intellectual functioning. This kind of programming strategy ignores the complex interrelationship that exists between cognitive and affective development. Once a child is labeled as emotionally disturbed, it is assumed that behavior problems seen in school are not caused by academic failure, but rather that academic failure is the result of the inappropriate behavior.

Given this line of reasoning and the definitions given to emotional disturbance, educable mental retardation, and learning disabilities, if children are to be labeled it is essential that these labels accurately reflect the needs of the children who carry them. If not, the child labeled as emotionally disturbed, who, in fact, has specific academic needs, will not be receiving an appropriate education, but will instead become even more delayed in skill development. This, in turn, will heighten negative emotional responses toward school and learning in general. For those children labeled as emotionally disturbed, whose intellectual development is not impaired, an educational program that focuses primarily on correcting their behavior neglects teaching these children the academic skills and knowledge base required for success both in and out of school. An individualized educational program (I.E.P.) may be written for such children, as required by P.L. 94–142, but it will be written within the context of the philosophy and structure of the program in which the child is placed. The goals, objectives, and methods of instruction prescribed for each child will correspond to preconceived notions regarding the child's needs, based on the label that has been assigned rather than on a truly objective assessment of that child.

The identification of children as learning disabled, educable mentally retarded or emotionally disturbed, and the subsequent programs developed for these children rely largely on the subjective judgments of educators. The U.S. General Accounting Office (1981) has found that there are a number of factors that influence a child's referral to special education other than the characteristics of the child. These include the eligibility criteria used in different school districts, program availability and timeliness, and the personal discretion of teachers and parents. This illustrates the validity of both the deviancy and ecological perspectives toward labeling, which point out that the designation of a child as disturbed is the end product of a complex interaction between that child and the social systems of which he or she is a part.

There are, however, objectively observable characteristics among the majority of those children who come to be identified as either learning disabled, educable mentally retarded, or emotionally disturbed. One is their sex. A 1981 study by the U. S. General Accounting Office demonstrated that there is a preponderance of males in each of these categories, with boys outnumbering girls three to one among those identified as emotionally disturbed. Black children are most overrepresented among students identified as educable mentally retarded, and are also, although less significantly, overrepresented among those labeled as emotionally disturbed. Although the majority of students labeled as learning disabled are also male, Blacks appear to be underrepresented in this category.

An official explanation has not been offered for the above. The Office of Civil Rights in the U.S. Department of Education describes these designations as conditions that rely heavily on the subjective judgments of administrators and teachers and suggests that the overrepresentation of males and Blacks as educable mentally retarded and emotionally disturbed may be the result of teacher/administrator bias related to the perception of what behaviors are normal. Certainly, it is possible to conclude, as has the General Accounting Office, that some of the overrepresentation of both males and Blacks as handicapped may be the result of other etiological factors, such as the greater vulnerability of male infants to many kinds of physiological stresses and the poor nutritional intake of low-income children and their mothers during pregnancy. However, from both a deviancy and an ecological perspective, there is clear evidence from these data that many societal biases, as reflected by our school system, may account for the disproportionate numbers of both Blacks and males among those children identified as emotionally disturbed.

Classroom teachers are the primary source of referrals to Committees on the Handicapped of children who later become identified as emotionally disturbed. Children who exhibit acting-out, disruptive behaviors are the ones most frequently referred. Prior to P.L. 94–142, many of these children were thought of as discipline problems. They were the "bad" kids who were always being punished, kept after school, held back a grade or two, or, when all else failed, expelled. Many classroom teachers were capable of managing difficult children in their classrooms, while others were constantly distressed by the management problems these children presented. In either case, the classroom teacher was seen as the person responsible for both educating and disciplining the disruptive child, just as he or she was for any other child in his or her charge.

P.L. 94–142's definition of emotional disturbance has provided an explanation for these children's behavior that removes the responsibility of managing such children from the classroom teacher. The child is now seen as "sick," and in need of "special education." This is not meant to imply that things were better in the "old days." Certainly, teachers should have been given support for the management of difficult children, and these children should not have been expelled from school. What is being questioned is whether or not, as far as the disturbing child is concerned, anything has really changed. Then and now, the problem was seen as residing within the child. No formal recognition has ever been given to the fact that disruptive behaviors in classrooms may, in part, be the result of the interactions that occur within those classrooms. They are not the sole responsibility of the child.

Ross (1980) found that "when it is recognized that the definition of disordered behavior depends on the expectations of those in the child's environment, it becomes clear that one must consider not only the demands thus made on the child, but also the tolerance level of this environment for behavior in its various forms" (p. 15). Since disruptive behaviors may now be defined as symptoms of a handicapping condition, and, therefore, not the responsibility of regular classroom teachers, teachers' tolerance for misbehavior may actually have lessened from what it had been prior to the enactment of P.L. 94–142. This, in turn, has resulted in a different pattern of interaction between teachers and disturbing children than would have been the case if these behaviors had continued to be perceived as normal childishness.

Teachers have always had expectations for their students' behavior and academic achievement. Often, these are based on the student's social class (Becker, 1952; Ogbu, 1974; Rist, 1970, 1973), sex (Ross, 1980; Schlosser & Algozzine, 1979; Werry & Quay, 1971), race (Crowe & MacGinite, 1974; Rubovits & Maehr, 1974), attractiveness (Ross & Salvia, 1975) and label of exceptionality (Foster, Ysseldyke & Reese, 1975; Gillung & Rucker, 1977; Salvia & Meisels, 1980; Vacc & Keist, 1977; Ysseldyke & Foster, 1978). In their classrooms, teachers may often act in ways that move students toward conformity with these expectations. Rist and Harrell (1982) have described this process in the following way:

1. The teacher expects specific behavior and achievement from a specific student.
2. Because of these different expectations, the teacher behaves differently towards the different students.
3. This teacher treatment tells each student what behavior and achievement the teacher expects; it affects the student's self-concept, achievement motivation, and level of aspiration.
4. If this teacher treatment is consistent over time, and if the student does not actively resist or change it in some way, it will tend to shape the student's achievement and behavior.
5. With time, the student's achievement and behavior will conform more and more closely to the original expectation. (p. 155)

The labeling of children as emotionally disturbed is one possible outcome of this kind of interaction between teachers and students. When, for example, a teacher expects that a Black, male student from a low-income, single parent family will be aggressive and defiant as well as poorly prepared for academic tasks, the same kinds of academic and social demands may not be placed on this child as on a middle-class child in the same classroom. Children quickly sense this differential treatment and may use their teacher's reluctance to confront them to what they believe to be their own advantage. Sensing the teacher's hesitancy, the child may even "act out" more often and thus avoid difficult academic tasks, while at the same time gaining status among his peers. If the teacher believes that the child's disruptive behaviors are symptoms of a handicapping condition then he or she may be even more reluctant to deal with the child directly. Instead, the child may be referred to the Committee on the Handicapped.

The data presented in this book will offer illustrations of the above scenario. In this study, "disturbed" behavior is the end product of a complex interaction that has occurred in the classroom. In addition, the evidence will suggest that teachers are not the sole source of expectations regarding a child's performance in school. In addition, as Finn (1972) suggests, an "expectation network" will be shown to exist. This network includes the expectations of teachers, peers, and the self-expectations of the pupils themselves; the classroom setting (which includes physical and psychological properties of the classroom, as well as the quantity and types of its materials); and out-of-school influences, which exert considerable influence on a child's behavior.

The labeling of children as emotionally disturbed must therefore be understood within the context of this total educational environment. Once a child is labeled, the expectation network found in this environment does not shut down. Rather, it is now expanded to include the definitions of emotional disturbance held by teachers, peers, the labeled child, the child's family, the community, and school officials. These definitions will interact and effect the types of educational programs offered. This includes the possibility of integrating, or "mainstreaming," the labeled child in regular classrooms.

The data that have been gathered for this study present the opportunity to explore the process of labeling children as deviant within its social context. A good deal has been written about this process as it has occurred with adults who have been labeled as mentally ill (Becker, 1963; Hollinshead & Redlich, 1958; Laing, 1967; Rosenhan, 1973; Scheff, 1966, 1974; Szasz, 1966). One has seen how, historically, women (Chesler, 1972), Blacks (Malzberg, 1965; Parker & Kleiner, 1966; Szasz, 1974), and individuals of low socioeconomic status (Strole & Fischer, 1971) appear to be overrepresented in the population of those considered to be insane. The field of special education has become increasingly concerned about the disproportionate number of minority and/or male children it serves (Dunn, 1968; Hobbs, 1975, 1976; Hurley, 1966; Jones, 1976; Mercer, 1973; Reynolds & Birch, 1977; Sarason & Doris, 1979). Most of this concern has been focused on the labeling of children as mentally retarded. There has been a growing concern about the use of emotional disturbance as a label that provides an administrative device to deal with minority children whose behavior does not fit the demands and expectations of school systems. However, research has not been directed at validating such concern. This can, in part, be explained by the fact that the identification of someone as disturbed is a complex phenomenon that involves more than the child and the labeler. It is a subjective judgment that involves the systems in which both operate, and the interactions between them. By following an ecological perspective, this study will explore the systems that have been involved in the labeling of children as emotionally disturbed in the city of Lakeside, and therefore add to the understanding of the transactional nature of the labeling process.

On the Present Study: Design and Content

I began gathering data for this study in March 1980, as a researcher on a National Institute for Education project (N.I.E. Grant #400-79-0052) designed to investigate programs that integrated handicapped children with non-handicapped children in typical public schools. The programs that had been nominated were thought of as representing exemplary mainstreaming practices. The project's aim was to disseminate information gathered from these programs, with the eventual goal of facilitating mainstreaming elsewhere. I studied the only program of the 25 selected for the N.I.E. project that included children identified as emotionally disturbed.

In fact, this program did not meet the project's criteria for selection. Nomination by two or more individuals (e.g., parents, teachers, administrators, school district personnel, university professors) in the county under study was required. Programs were then selected that represented a variety of handicapping conditions. The Education Center at the Medgar Evers School (pseudonym) received only one such nomination, but was included in order for the project to present successful mainstreaming practices for "disturbed" children.

I was to discover that categorizing Evers as a typical public school did not accurately represent reality. Evers is not typical, but is, rather, a typical urban ghetto school. Located in the predominantly Black section of a midsized, northeastern city (hereafter referred to as "Lakeside"), Evers' school-age population in 1981 was 94 percent Black. Over half its children lived in single-parent, female-headed households and/or received some sort of public assistance. All the children received free or reduced-fee lunch and breakfast (Eligibility for the lunch and breakfast programs required that a child's family fall at or below the minimum income level established by the federal government.) Their families represented the substantial numbers of Black Americans whose economic and social status had not changed significantly from what it had been 20 years before.

Like that of many other modern ghetto schools, Evers' physical appearance reinforces an image of order and responsiveness to the community. Some may find psychological comfort in having a shiny new building named after a martyred civil rights leader, closing of school on Martin Luther King's birthday, and the celebration of Black Americans month. However, such symbolic changes have significantly altered neither the life of the poor, Black urban family nor the ethnocentric perspectives of many of the teachers at Evers and other schools in this community. These teachers' descriptions of children from low-income families, whether Black or White, are presented in negative images. Poor families are seen primarily in terms of their deficiencies.

The Evers staff consistently expressed the opinion that, as a consequence of their backgrounds, students there were more aggressive, less organized, and more academically behind than were their middle-class White contemporaries. They were seen as needing a more "highly structured" learning environment, as well as a good deal more discipline and nurturing than might be found at other, predominantly White elementary schools. The ability of the Evers staff to program for children who had been labeled "severely emotionally disturbed" (S.E.D.) was clearly related to the definition the staff had given its "typical" students. Both groups were children from low-income families and most lived in single-parent families. Of those labeled S.E.D., 80 percent were Black and all were boys.

All but three of the 34 students in the Education Center in March 1980 who were labeled severely emotionally disturbed had been sent to Evers from racially integrated, "middle-class" schools where, as a consequence of their behavior, they came to be identified as disturbed. The middle-class nature of the schools that had referred these children did not always relate to the socioeconomic makeup of the other students; several schools in the city also had large numbers of impoverished students. However, the staff at these schools were described by teachers and other members of the staff at Evers as well as by school district officials as having a lower tolerance for verbal confrontation, "foul" language, physical contact, or general defiance by students than did teachers at Evers. It was not that Evers teachers made allowances for these kinds of inappropriate behaviors, but, rather, that they had come to expect that their typical students would behave in these kinds of ways. As a result, behaviors seen as deviant elsewhere were seen as normal at Evers.

In fact, Evers referred fewer students for special education placement than any other school in the city of Lakeside. Its teachers had learned to attach a different meaning to the "negative" behavior of Black, male children than did teachers at other schools. Although Evers' teachers did believe that the inappropriate behavior of their students was the outcome of inadequate socialization, these behaviors were not viewed as symptoms of illness. Rather, the typical Evers student and the students labeled severely emotionally disturbed who had been sent to Evers from other schools were regarded as children who had not been taught the social skills necessary for success in school. Evers' teachers believed that their job included the teaching of these skills.

How did the Evers staff arrive at this understanding of their students' behavior? What were the consequences? How could a racially segregated school such as this exist so openly in the 1980s? And, how could students be labeled as severely emotionally disturbed when, in fact, many people did not believe that these children were "mentally ill"? This book attempts to answer these questions. The adoption of an ethnographic approach provided the vehicle for unravelling the complex nature of these issues.

I spent between two and three hours a day, at different times of the day and on different days of the week, in each of Evers' special education classes. I also did extensive observations in regular classrooms in which special education students were being mainstreamed, as well as observing at least one additional classroom for each grade level. I did not wish to record specific teaching techniques in each setting, but rather, for purposes of comparison, to focus on the interactions between teachers and students, and those between the students themselves. I was also interested in the ways the teachers organized their classrooms. In this way, I was able to compare the physical environment and organization of daily activities in the special education classrooms with those in the regular classrooms.

Data were also gathered by questioning significant people in the school. This questioning process took two forms. The first was an informal discussion of an individual's perspective on the organization as a whole, his or her specific role, the children at the school, the neighborhood, mainstreaming, and/or whatever else might seem relevant to the situation we were experiencing. These informal talks took place as events in the school were unfolding; thus, discussions frequently involved several individuals and myself.

The second form of questioning involved semistructured interviews, conducted on a one-to-one basis, in private, with individuals connected to the school by diverse roles and associations. These discussions often took place in addition to the more informal conversations I might have had with the same person while we were involved with other people, or while we were observing a particular event. These interviews, although more formal than the previously described discussions, were not question and answer periods. They were private conversations, often tape recorded, during which I tried to discover the subject's perspectives on the school as a whole, his or her perceived role(s), and, in my preliminary work for the N.I.E. study, his or her understanding of the mainstreaming process.

I interviewed as many regular teachers as I could talk to on a one-to-one basis (six regular classroom teachers, as well as two teachers in the preschool program). I also interviewed the school's social worker, two principals, nurse, reading specialist, resource teacher, "school–community aide," teacher aides (two), instructional specialist, two school psychologists, special education teachers (three), mainstreamed students (four), and the social worker assigned to work in the school's special education programs. In addition, I had more informal conversations with aides, cafeteria workers, gym and music teachers, the librarian, custodians, school secretaries, and many of the children, whom I would meet in the cafeteria, principal's office, social worker's office, resource room, playground, classrooms, and even in the hallways.

The Medgar Evers School is a real place and the data reported in this study are factual accounts. However, in order to protect the anonymity of the school, its personnel, the children and families discussed, and the many individuals interviewed, names have been changed and identities concealed. It has been necessary, in some instances, to change individuals' job titles. This has been done only when a person's title would clearly identify him or her. Only in those cases where knowing a person's specific role was essential to understanding his or her point of view were actual job titles given. For example, it is important to our understanding of the labeling process, as it has occurred in Lakeside, to know that a psychiatrist is the person responsible for the official designation of a student as emotionally disturbed. He presents a point of view that relates to his professional training. That is not to say that *all* psychiatrists believe as he does, nor would they necessarily behave in the manner presented here. Rather, because the medical model is inherent in his professional identity, knowing his actual title adds to our understanding of his perspectives.

The sex and race of the people described in this study have not been changed, although doing so would certainly have helped to conceal their identities. What emerged from the data gathered in this study indicates that we can best understand the events that took place in Lakeside and its schools from the early 1960s to the present by knowing the race and sex of the participants in these events. For example, relevant to our understanding of the changes that occurred at Evers during the late 1970s is the knowledge that the principals during those years were Black women who grew up in this city. As mothers of children who attended the Lakeside schools, they were additionally sensitive to the treatment of Black children in Lakeside's schools.

It became apparent that the culture of the Evers school had not developed out of deliberate or conscious malice toward its students. Nor had the labeling of disruptive students come about simply as an expeditious method of dealing with troublesome behavior. Referring teachers genuinely believed that placement in a special education program would help these students. Understanding these phenomena required an unravelling of the complex social and political forces that had impacted upon the city of Lakeside and its entire school district during the past 20 years. Evers, like every other school in this country, was only one small part of a larger "ecosystem" (Bronfenbrenner, 1976).

To better understand both the relationship of this school to the larger school system, and the process by which students became identified as emotionally disturbed, I conducted interviews with individuals outside the school building, in different positions in the school district's bureaucracy. These included an assistant superintendent, the director of pupil services, the school district psychiatrist, the director of special education, the chairperson of the district's Committee on the Handicapped, the district's director of research, and the head of its food programs. In addition, I was given access to documents that related to reading levels throughout the district, the racial and socioeconomic makeup of the city schools, and the district's busing program. I was also able to look into past minutes of the district's school board meetings that related to Evers' history, as well as to the debates surrounding the issue of racial integration.

It became apparent that both the Evers school and the Education Center needed to be viewed not only in the context of the city school district, but also as a part of the history of the city's Black community. Interviews with

Black parents and community members, the head of the City Housing Commission, the former editor of a local Black newspaper and a current member of the Lakeside Development Corporation, the school district's community workers, as well as informal conversations with numerous individuals, Black and White, who have lived in this city for from ten to 50 years, suggested that the racial and socioeconomic makeup of the children who had been labeled emotionally disturbed were, indeed, significant.

This book will describe what I learned during the year spent researching the Lakeside city schools, the Evers school in particular, and, finally, the Education Center and its students, all of whom were boys labeled as severely emotionally disturbed. In the next chapter, our understanding of the school will be broadened by first exploring the city of Lakeside and its Black community. The school can then be understood in the context of this city and its response to the massive immigration of poor and working-class Blacks from the South during the 1950s and 1960s.

The Evers school and its evolution over the past 20 years will be described in Chapter 4. The ways that teachers at Evers today relate to their students, which includes a tolerance for behaviors that are perceived as symptoms of emotional disturbance at other Lakeside elementary schools, will be seen as related to the events that occurred in the Ever's neighborhood during the 1960s. Federal and state mandates to integrate the city's schools in the 1960s and 1970s will be shown to have had a significant impact both on this particular school and on the overall development of programs for children from low-income, minority families.

In 1972, the Lakeside Community Action Agency (C.A.A.) contracted with the city school district to provide a program for "unserved youth," i.e., low-income children who had dropped out, or had been thrown out, of school. Chapter 5 will describe how this program, the Education Center, evolved into a public school special education program for children labeled severely emotionally disturbed. The program, as it operated at Evers in 1981–82, will be described.

In Chapter 6, the process by which children in Lakeside became labeled as emotionally disturbed will be explored. The perspectives of those involved in the labeling process will be presented, as will specific documentation of how some children became labeled. Two children, Michael Thomas and Carl Smith, will then be introduced in Chapter 7. Both boys had been labeled as severely emotionally disturbed and placed in the Education Center. None of their teachers at Evers believed either of these boys to be "really disturbed." Their careers as students will be described, as will the consequences of their labeling. The implications of these data will then be explored in the final chapter.

3

The City of Lakeside

The "Black Community"

A northeastern industrial city with a population of between 150,000 and 200,000, Lakeside is a typical urban nucleus of a "standard metropolitan statistical area." Although relatively small when compared to the 85 largest cities in the United States, it is considered typical because of its proximity to rural and suburban areas, population density, per capita income level, diverse industrial base, employment distribution, and racial and ethnic composition. Approximately 16 percent of its citizens are Black.

Like most other northern urban metropolitan areas, Lakeside experienced rapid population growth between 1950 and 1970. Postwar industrialization, spurred on by military contracts to local industries; manufacturing; chemical, shipping, and freight companies; a growing university center; and a nearby Navy base attracted skilled, semiskilled, and unskilled workers to the area. The population growth experienced in the region during these years came from both the migration of workers to the area and the postwar baby boom.

From 1950 through 1970, a large percentage of the people who migrated to Lakeside were Black. In fact, during that period, the actual and percentage growth of the Black population in this city was one of the largest in the nation (see Table 3.1).[1] During those years, Lakeside's overall population was declining, while at the same time, an unprecedented rate of growth was seen in the rural and suburban areas outside the central city. Although in recent years the population both in the city and the surrounding region has declined, the numbers of Black citizens within the city continues to increase.

---

1. In gathering some of the historic and demographic data on the city of "Lakeside," secondary sources have been used. Because these sources might reveal the actual identity of this city, they have not been cited in the biliography. Instead, data such as that found in this table which have been gathered from secondary sources, are indicated by an asterisk (*).

TABLE 3.1
(Percent of Overall and Black Population Growth in Lakeside)

	Overall % Growth	Black % Growth
1970-80	− 17.8	24
1960-70	− 8.3	90.7
1950-60	− 2.1	144.4

Large portions of the incoming Black population had come directly from the South or had been born in the South and lived elsewhere before coming to Lakeside. The bulk of the Black population, therefore, constituted a new community. As a consequence of their newness to Lakeside, southern Blacks had little awareness of politics in the city. The culture shock of settling into a northern, urban environment, as well as economic pressures, would combine to make the new migrants particularly vulnerable to the political manipulations that were to follow. The political events in Lakeside that followed the mass migration of southern Blacks directly influenced both the type of environment in which many Black children were to be raised (i.e., public housing projects in a decaying neighborhood) and the kind of education they would receive (i.e., segregated schools that operated under a set of expectations concerning the perceived "needs" of Black children).

Blacks had lived in Lakeside since before the Civil War. In fact, this city was a stop on the Underground Railroad and the site of much Abolitionist activity. In spite of this, the Black population remained at about one percent until the 1940s, when it more than doubled. The opening of a Navy base and the expansion of many war-related industries offered new employment opportunities. Many southern Blacks were also familiar with the rural regions surrounding Lakeside, having previously been agricultural migrant workers.

They would quickly discover that the Black community that existed prior to their arrival had accommodated itself to northern-style discrimination by concentrating in the section of the city where Blacks were permitted to rent and by holding the kinds of jobs that were available to them. Although relations between Whites and Blacks had historically been friendly, discrimination in employment was widespread, and Blacks had found work primarily in unskilled jobs, as domestics, laborers, and waiters. Attempts by Black professionals to establish themselves in Lakeside had been repeatedly thwarted. A local newspaper, for example, reported the following story in 1905:

> Charles E. Toney, colored, a graduate of the College of Law of Lakeside University last spring, sub-rented an office in the Kirk block a few days ago.

Today he was notified that he couldn't have it. It is reported that when Henry Lyon, agent of the Kirk block, heard of this transaction, he took steps toward evicting the colored lawyer on the grounds that the other tenants on the block would be opposed to having a colored man there.*

Discrimination in both housing and employment continued throughout the twentieth century, becoming more overt during those times when migration of Blacks increased. One such period occurred during World War I, when the opening of munitions plants in the city presented Blacks with the opportunity for employment. A local newspaper printed the following report in 1917:

> The influx of Southern Negroes is becoming serious in Lakeside. While many of them have gone to larger cities, at least 150 and probably many more located within the city within the last two months. They are looking for work and although laborers are needed, many people will not employ Negroes because their White laborers quit rather than work with them.*

Although the overt discrimination that had previously existed in Lakeside was less evident after World War II and the years that followed, the unprecedented numbers of Blacks who moved to this region would not find the city to be the promised land they had hoped for. Whites were abandoning the inner city and leaving behind slum conditions and increased unemployment. The new Black community that followed had no cohesiveness, was naive in the ways of urban politics, and was generally concerned with individual survival.

There is little evidence that a cohesive Black community exists in Lakeside today. There is no recognized leadership from the church, as is often the case in Black communities. There are several Black churches and many "Reverends" vying for leadership, but none that has emerged as a unifying force. Certainly the newness of the community is an important factor, but so too is the historic discrimination against Blacks in this city. There is no established community of Black professionals or business people. In fact, Lakeside has a negligible number of Black business people and few Black professionals. Although this city has a major law school and medical school, the legal and medical services available in the area where the largest percentage of Blacks live were, in 1981, limited to the neighborhood offfice of one elderly general practitioner.

When Black people in Lakeside speak of the "Black community" here, they are most often referring to the neighborhood surrounding the Evers school. Whites mistakenly assume that this geographic community represents a psychological community as well (one woman put it, " White folks think we all think alike"). The individuals and families who live here are, for the most part, struggling on their own, psychologically isolated from one another. Unlike the days of the civil rights movement or the War on Poverty, today problems of survival are seen as problems facing individuals. They are not perceived as collective concerns.

The Evers Neighborhood

The five census tracts immediately surrounding Evers, containing the attendance area from which its students are drawn, have a population that is 77 percent Black. The census tract in which the school building is located is 85 percent Black. Examination of the population trends in Lakeside over the past 20 years reveals that the density of the Black population has increased in these areas. The two adjacent tracts to the immediate west of Evers have become disproportionately populated by Blacks during the past ten years. The general identification of the "West Side" as a Black community has created an expansion of Black population into neighborhoods in this direction. Because Whites living west of the Black community of ten years ago feared an influx of Blacks, they sold or rented their homes quickly, creating the very situation they feared was inevitable.

Knowing only that the Black population of the city is highly concentrated around Evers tells only about the complexion of the community. However, when one realizes that Black poverty is even more highly concentrated in these same areas, it becomes evident that the issues confronting Evers have as much to do with social class as with race. Looking at 1970 census data, one can see that although the citywide rate of poverty was approximately 14 percent, the average rate of poverty for Blacks within the five census tracts surrounding Evers was 34 percent. This section of the city continues to have a higher concentration of poor people in general, and an even higher concentration of poor Blacks, than does the city as a whole.

Segregated neighborhoods have a long history in Lakeside. During the first part of this century, Blacks lived in a section of the city known both as "the Zone" and "Jew Town." Within this area, ethnic groups maintained their separate ways of life. As the years went by, however, members of other ethnic groups moved up and out of "the Zone." Large numbers of Jews remained, both because of anti-Semitism and the desire of the Jewish community to remain near each other and their synagogue. The area is still referred to by oldtimers as "Jew Town." Karen Mitchell, a Black woman and former principal at Evers, recalled her life growing up in "Jew Town" and the changes she saw occur during the 1940s and 1950s:

> When I was a girl we lived in the section of the city called "Jew Town." It was called that because for years it was the only section of town where Jews lived.

I remember that we all got along pretty well, went to the same schools and played together. It was also the only section of town where Blacks could rent. The Jews were the only ones who would rent to Blacks.

Well, as they became more affluent, they moved to the suburbs or to the South Side. A lot of homes were sold or rented. The neighborhood became mostly Black. Then, in the early sixties, "Urban Renewal" came in and wiped out all the houses. Do you know where the State Rehabilitation Center is? Well, that's the center of what used to be "Jew Town," across from where the Interstate and the Ramada Inn are located.

What happened in Lakeside in the early 1960s is typical of descriptions of the results of urban renewal efforts throughout the United States in cities of similar size and description. Residential areas housing predominantly poor, elderly, and minorities were leveled to allow for the construction of a municipal center, city library, modern office buildings, a rehabilitation facility, and the interstate highway. Between 1960 and 1970, approximately 4,000 Lakeside families were relocated, when possible, and/or given cash as compensation for their inconvenience or to help them establish new homes.

It was clear that there was not adequate housing in Lakeside in which to relocate all the people who were displaced by urban renewal. The numbers of Blacks migrating here was continuing at an unprecedented rate, putting additional pressure on the city's need for housing. The majority of these people could not afford to buy homes, nor would discriminatory practices have allowed it had they been able. Large numbers of the recent migrants were young people with, or soon to be with children, which would further swell their population.* The city responded to these needs by building public housing facilities. These units became segregated by both age and race, with separate public housing facilities constructed for senior citizens, and others for families. Racially segregated schools with large numbers of children developed in those neighborhoods into which Black families were relocated. Evers was one of these schools.

In trying to discover why the neighborhood surrounding Evers was chosen as the site for the construction of two large public housing units, I found that there was already a large public housing project in that neighborhood, which had been constructed in the late 1930s. These older units had become predominantly Black by 1960, increasing the out-migration of Whites from private homes in the area. Building two more large public housing complexes in the same neighborhood increased the density of poor, recently migrated Blacks. I wondered if those involved in the decision to build the housing projects in the Evers neighborhood realized that their plan would result in the creation of a ghetto.

A city housing commission spokesperson explained that this area was chosen precisely because it already had public housing in it: the people in the neighborhood were "used to it." In another neighborhood, particularly a White neighborhood, local residents would have been "up in arms." I asked if it had been anticipated that the projects would become predominantly Black. (The three public housing facilities are 99%, 92% and 98% Black.) He responded by saying:

> It's no accident. These people had mostly come from the South. They had never owned anything in their lives, so it wasn't so bad for them to be living in public housing. Now, the Whites were used to owning houses, even when they weren't such good houses. So they chose to live in private houses. Also the Blacks have a kinship system. They liked to stick together and support each other. They may not have made it out there on their own.

I questioned this man further about the fact that the city was operating segregated housing facilities and wondered if any attempt had been made recently to integrate, following the passage of Civil Rights legislation, given what is known about the negative social impact of segregated housing. "I wouldn't touch that with a ten-foot pole," he said, grinning. "That would be political suicide. Don't forget, we are providing better housing than these people would be able to get on their own."

My conversations with several individuals who have lived in the public housing units surrounding Evers, or who are living there now, indicate that there has been a shift in the attitudes of its occupants. Many residents in the 1950s and some in the early 1960s saw living in public housing as a temporary situation. Their hope was to work their way out of the projects and move into their own homes. Meanwhile, a sense of community developed, particularly in Frontier Homes, the older, two-storied, attached apartment units.

Greg Parnell is a teacher at the Evers school. He is a Black man in his mid-thirties, who moved to Lakeside from the South with his family when he was in junior high school, during the mid-1950's. They considered themselves fortunate to find housing in Frontier Homes. He found that in the years he was growing up, people related to each other and to each other's families in the way he had found they had in the South.

> I had a big family and initially when I went to school, I was in the South. And our family was very clannish-like and everybody knew everybody. Even other people outside the family was involved. If I was doing something wrong in the street, anybody, even a neighbor, could discipline me, beat me, feel free about it and then take me home. But that doesn't happen any more, particularly in cities. I know it still goes on in small communities in the South. Well, parents feel that everybody's out to get 'em. . . . When we lived in Frontier Homes, the

people that lived in the immediate area, like in the building and in that row housing, they were close. Now my mother could do a thing with other people's kids 'cause we would spend time in other people's houses and their parents would do a thing with us. People are afraid of each other now. The kids would fight 'em and I don't blame 'em for being afraid of the kids. When I worked at the community center, there were kids there, eleven, twelve, and thirteen years old who would beat on old Black women. That's why I think we've lost a lot. Black families used to be real close, but that's not true anymore.

Tommy Jones, the former editor of a now defunct Black newspaper and a current member of the Lakeside Development Corporation, expressed a similar opinion. He related the changes, however, not just to public housing, but to the neighborhood as a whole:

The neighborhood around Evers used to be real clannish, you know, folks looking out for one another. Even ten and fifteen years ago. I think that maybe what happened is that when folks began to make it, they'd move away, out of the neighborhood. Then the new Southern Blacks began moving in. They're more industrial. Maybe they'd lived in Southern cities, but they weren't folks who were used to owning things. So you get those folks and the people who are stuck in public housing. These are the drudges, folks who see welfare and public housing as a way of life, not as a temporary thing. Like Poppa Dad used to say, "The best crab will crawl out of the barrel." You couldn't keep a Tommy Jones in public housing.

There is general agreement that in the 1950s and early 1960s the residents of the neighborhood surrounding Evers, particularly those who lived in the public housing projects, provided each other with the psychosocial supports essential for a viable community. Unfortunately, many of the current occupants of the housing projects do not feel that support coming from the community in which they live.

Althea Clarence is a single mother, 25 years old. She and her three sons, ages nine, seven and four, live in Middle Village, one of the larger housing projects built in the early 1960s. They are supported by public assistance, i.e., Aid to Families with Dependent Children and Supplemental Social Security. Her nine-year-old son is deaf. She says:

I've lived in this neighborhood all my life and it's gone through a lot of changes. We lived in Frontier Homes, my momma and nine of us kids. Later on my stepfather was there and there were nine kids. So we had to move from Frontier Homes to Middle Village. That's where I live with my kids and I'm trying to get out and back into Frontier Homes. See, Middle Village is no good. The people there have big families and it's all women and kids. There are gangs of them kids and no one pays 'em any mind. They steal stuff and make a lot of noise. Why, you can't even hang your clothes out anymore 'cause they get stolen right off the line. And the cops won't come into the projects. They scared and I don't blame 'em. And you can't say nothin' to anybody about their kids messin' around. They think everybody is out to get 'em and are real jealous if you gets anything for yourself. Frontier Homes is better. The apartments are smaller, so there are less kids and more men around too. It's kept up better.

Although Althea Clarence is correct in saying the apartments in Frontier Homes are somewhat smaller than those in Middle Village, her image of the culture of the latter may be a reflection of her childhood memories of the projects. Today the two housing projects resemble each other totally, in terms of the distribution of residents by age, sex, income, and race, as illustrated in Table 3.2.

Although Table 3.2 clearly indicates that both housing projects are occupied predominantly by female-headed households, it is doubtful that the numbers presented give an accurate picture of the situations that actually exist for each family. Statistics such as these rarely include individuals who live with the family but are not related by blood or marriage. This information is often hidden from official scrutiny to protect welfare payment and/ or to keep common-law relationships invisible to potentially disapproving housing authority officials. Although the 82 percent and 84 percent figures may represent an overestimate of the actual number of single-parent families, it is clear that large numbers of the children in Frontier Homes and Middle Village live in situations that are different from the idealized two-parent nuclear family.

Most residents of both housing projects, as well as individuals who are frequent visitors there, do not differentiate between the two in the way that Althea does. Rather, the picture generally painted of the projects is that of a ghetto environment, i.e., it is perceived as an area that houses the Black underclass.Tilly Post, a woman employed by the Lakeside public schools as their community worker, is one person who described the housing projects in that way. Her job includes acting as an spokesperson for parents who feel that their children are not receiving adequate education services. A Black

TABLE 3.2
Public Housing Demographics, January 1981

	Total Tenant Pop.	% Black	% Female H.O.H.†	% Age 0-20*	% H.O.H. Employed
Frontier Homes	1126	98.5	82	84	35
Middle Village	1110	98	84	88	40

†H.O.H. = Head of Household
*H.O.H. in this age range not included here, only dependents.

woman in her early forties, Tilly came here 17 years ago from Atlanta, Georgia, when her husband entered graduate school at Lakeside University. She is often pessimistic about the possibilities for Blacks in this city. She feels, in general, that "this is not the town to raise Black kids in." She has chosen to send her own two children to Catholic schools in this city, despite the expense and the fact that neither she nor her husband is Catholic. She feels that, in general, teachers in Lakeside hold low expectations for Black students.

Tilly is particularly distressed over the life she sees in public housing. She feels that many of the women there have given up, choosing to sit at home, watch soap operas and wait for their welfare checks: "Living in public housing, the people don't get to see anything else or learn any other way of life. They see despair, apathy and hopelessness, and pass it on to their kids." Unlike Tilly Post's perspective on the negative effects of public housing on the lives of these families, others interviewed for this study, from all walks of life and from both racial groups, tended to focus on the shortcomings of individuals who, they feel, are responsible for their own poverty and lack of skills.

This perspective fails to recognize the significance of the fact that the majority of the residents of the projects are single mothers and their children. The economic realities facing these families are worse than they were 20 years ago. In addition, the young, single Black mother still faces the double jeopardy of racism and sexism. The following incident reported by a young White woman who recently gave birth to her first child at the State Medical Center Hospital illustrates that these biases may begin to impact on the single Black mother and her baby even before they leave the hospital:

There was a young Black girl in the bed next to mine who had just had her first baby too. She couldn't have been more than sixteen years old. I couldn't help but compare my life to hers and how different our children's lives were going to be, even from the beginning. First of all, she was very scared. Not only was she in a great deal of pain, but she had to go through the whole experience alone. Her mother wanted to be with her, but they insisted that hospital practice only allowed for the father to be in the labor or delivery room. The worst part was that this poor girl needed to be catheterized and even when she rang for the nurses, they wouldn't come like they would for me. One time, her bag needed changing and no one came, so it spilled all over the floor. When they did come, the nurse yelled at her. When they would bring in the babies, all the nurses would fuss over my girl and no one paid any attention to hers. She finally broke down and cried one night and told me she was in pain, but was afraid to ask for medication because the last time she had asked, the nurse called her a baby and told her to remember the pain the next time she thought about getting pregnant.

As in the case of refusing permission for anyone other than the baby's father to be admitted into the labor and delivery rooms, many public policies operate under definitions of situations that represent a covert form of discrimination. Definitions of the intact family as consisting of both parents, with the father as head of this nuclear unit, have, for many years, resulted in policies that have discriminated against the large numbers of Black families that have operated as female-headed units.

It is important to remember that this neighborhood is not exclusively public housing, and that not all the families in the projects or in private homes have given up the struggle to improve their lives. Most of the private homes in Lakeside are two- and three-storied wood-frame structures, approximately 60 or more years old. Some have ornate porches and other classic Victorian type architectural features decorating their facades. The most visible evidence of positive activity are the renovations of many of the neighborhood's older homes that were either abandoned or have fallen into disrepair. The Lakeside Development Corporation has identified the residential area to the immediate west and north of Evers as a neighborhood they will provide with funds and technical assistance for property improvements.

The Medgar Evers School

From the adjacent parking lot, one gets a sense of the patchwork history of both the neighborhood and the school. What is today the rear of the building was, 60 years ago, the entire school. This three-story, red stone building, once called the Quincy School, is hidden from view when one enters its main front entrance. (The Education Center classes were located in this back section from 1977 through 1980.) Behind it, two large smoke-stacks of a steam plant pump exhaust fumes into the air. Abandoned shops surround the plant. Leaving the parking lot and walking to the front of the building, one passes the more modern three-storied, red brick middle wing, which connects the old building to an even newer one, with a modern facade. Nearby, cars speed overhead on the interstate highway that passes through the neighborhood.

Walking along the path that leads to the front of the building's double-doored glass entrance, one is likely to be struck by the contrast between the modern appearance of the new wing and the view from the rear of the old building. A modern architectural rendition of an old stone wall runs between the path and the modernistic two-story gray brick and formed concrete structure, renamed in the late 1960s as the Medgar Evers School. The name of the martyred civil rights leader appears in foot-high, stainless steel letters on the opposite side of the building, which faces Middle Village, the public housing project built in the early 1960s. A playground, located between this side of the building and the projects, contains spaceship-like play equipment, in need of paint. Grass now pushes its way through cracks at the base of three large concrete forms whose purpose has been forgotten. The large yard surrounding the playground is circled by a low fence and shut but unlocked gates, which seem intended more to keep children safely inside than to keep others out.

Over each of the windows in the front of the building are huge concrete awning-like structures. The majority of windows in the building are not glass, but a translucent plastic covered by a crisscross of heavy wire mesh. Several people from outside the community have pointed out that the windows, concrete forms and stone wall in front create the appearance of a fortress. It is particularly relevant that the impression of Evers held by those who have little if any contact with it is that of a tough, inner-city ghetto school. Merely visiting, let alone working there, is seen by outsiders as a risk of life and limb. Evers' teachers are continually being asked, "Aren't you afraid of getting mugged in that school?" Although Evers certainly is an inner-city ghetto school, the perception of it as dangerous reflects nothing of the reality I experienced between March 1980 and March 1981.

The majority of teachers I spoke with both at Evers and at three other Lakeside schools described the typical Evers student as highly aggressive, disorganized, and academically unprepared. Their lack of readiness for school was most often associated with what was believed to be the inadequate socialization they had received at home. Single mothers were the most frequent focus of attack. Certainly the average Evers student was behind the average Lakeside student, as far as reading and math achievement were concerned. However, as I spent more and more time in the building, I began to wonder about the image that had been presented regarding the children's social behavior.

I observed children in the hallways, talking quietly and, often, affectionately to one another. It was commonplace to see an "older" sibling (eight or nine years old) bring a younger brother or sister to one of the prekindergarten programs in the school or wait to take him or her home at the end of the day. The older child might, typically, give some information to the teacher or school nurse, kiss the younger child, and remind him or her to "mind" the teacher. The cafeteria, although certainly noisy, filled with the chatter of small children and adults, never hit the deafening pitch I have found in many other elementary school lunchrooms. The same seemed true of the children's behavior on the playground.

Where were all these highly aggressive and disorganized ghetto youngsters that both the staff and others outside the school had described? Could it be that the highly structured behavioral approach that was followed at Evers was working and I was witnessing the success of that program? Another possibility presented itself, and its likelihood was reinforced in an interview I had with the Ever's school psychologist, Dick Hunter. A White man in his early thirties, he had worked for the school district for six years and spent time in a dozen school buildings other than Evers. I asked him to try to compare the behavior of the students here with that of kids of the same age at other schools:

Mr. Hunter: The kids are much the same.

Question: What about aggressive behavior? I have heard a lot of people say that it's easier to mainstream emotionally disturbed kids here who are aggressive because they're not that different from the rest of the kids in the school.

Mr. Hunter: If you approach it in any way with some objectivity, I think it would be easy to classify this building as the same as most others in the city, as far as aggressive behavior is concerned. There may be some exceptions, like in one or two of the smaller, very upper-middle class schools, but for the majority of kids, certainly in the district, and for those schools which represent the majority of the district, the behavior of the kids in this school are not that different. There may be a difference in the minds of the people who work in the building, and possibly in the minds of those who work at other schools. They would say, "Oh yes, the behavior at Evers is worse, more aggressive."

Question: Are you saying that it is more how people look at the school than what's really going on here?

Mr. Hunter: Yes.

What Dick was saying is supported by the findings of much of the literature that has studied the interaction of teacher expectations and the education of Black children (Becker, 1970; Henry, 1971; Leacock, 1969; Ogbu, 1974; Rist, 1970, 1973; Ryan, 1971; Silverstein & Krate, 1975). These authors found that teachers often based their academic and social programs on preconceived ideas about the learning styles and the academic/social potential of children.

The staff at Evers, like others in Lakeside, have developed a perspective toward their students based both on their stereotypical fears of Blacks and from the experiences they have had in past years. A culture has developed at this school based on these perceptions that is believed to be responsive to the needs of today's students, but that may instead reflect these fears and past events. The late 1960s and early 1970s were years of upheaval in the education of Black children in Lakeside. In order to better understand the images held by the Evers staff today, and the program that followed from these images, one must look closely at the school during the turbulence of the 1960s and 1970s.

The Evers school, as seen today, is the product of an evolution that occurred in this school, in this northeastern city, over the past 20 years. The changes that occurred here can be viewed as a series of events that paralleled changes in federal policy as well as broader societal changes. This examination is by no means a complete history, but is rather an exploration of events and policies that helped shape Evers. Events have been identified as significant by individuals who have been involved with this school and its surrounding community during all or part of the past 20 years. These events will be seen to have been important in this school's development and will clarify our understanding of how Black children came to be overidentified as severely emotionally disturbed in this city.

4

The Medgar Evers School

The 1960s

The early 1960s mark the beginning of massive federal government intervention into the problems facing the poor. Funds were allocated for public housing and the construction of new schools. In 1961, the newest wing of the Evers school was constructed, aided by such funds. During the 1950s the unprecedented growth of the Black population in this city, which was concentrated in this neighborhood, resulted in the addition of a new wing to the existing 60-year-old Quincy School. The construction of additional public housing projects in 1961 across the street from the school made the addition of a third wing necessary in order to accommodate the children who would be living in the projects.

A report titled, "K–6 Racial Census by School (1962–1980)," compiled by the Lakeside City School District shows Evers moved from being predominantly Black in 1962 (68%) to being almost exclusively Black in 1966 (92%). The public housing project put in this neighborhood to accommodate relocated Black families solidified the segregated nature of this community, thereby creating truly segregated education for its children.

In the 1950s and early 1960s, the federal government's attack on segregated schools was focused primarily on the South. Northerners were, for the most part, complacent about their school systems. The neighborhood school was perceived as providing for the needs of the children in their own geographically immediate areas. The reality of the situation was that often, as in the case of Lakeside, the "choice" of neighborhood had been made for Black families by both discriminatory housing practices and their relocation into public housing. Schools in these neighborhoods, such as Evers, reflected this choice.

Beginning in 1965, the federal government provided funds through the Elementary and Secondary Education Act to such schools, i.e., those with significant concentrations of students from low-income backgrounds. Unfortunately, little was known about establishing effective programs for these children (Wayson, 1975). Programs and policies reflected preconceived notions regarding the needs and desires of low-income people, and, because of this, often failed to benefit those the programs sought to serve (Rainwater & Yancy, 1967). The thrust of school programs for the poor, minority children was compensatory and directed at changing the child to fit into the values, attitudes and attributes of the dominant culture.

The fact that Blacks were not actively involved in either high level policy decision making, or in the development of educational programs at the local level in these early years at Evers can now be seen to have played a role in the failure of programs and policies that were developed without such participation. The establishment of a "magnet" program at Evers in 1967 as a means of racially integrating the school presents an excellent illustration of this phenomenon. In turn, the failure of this program provided evidence to school professionals that poor, Black children were not capable of benefiting from a "progressive, enriched" education. Families of Black children were additionally reinforced in their belief that it was useless to try to communicate with the school.

In March 1967, the Lakeside Board of Education met and proposed the Alternative Attendance Program, a voluntary busing plan aimed at achieving racial integration. This meeting was in direct response to an order from state and federal civil rights offices. This plan included the recommendation that, "Negro students, attending a school whose Negro enrollment is greater than 1.5 times the overall City School District racial percentage pattern at its particular educational level, should have the opportunity of transferring to a school whose Negro enrollment percentage is less than the overall City School District percentage pattern at its particular educational level." White students would also be "permitted" to transfer to any school whose "Negro enrollment percentage is greater than the overall City School District racial percentage pattern at its particular level."

There were 31 elementary schools in Lakeside in 1967, and of these, only five exceeded by 1.5 times the citywide Black enrollment percentage of 21 percent. However, none of the four other schools that would be affected by the plan was as totally segregated by race as was Evers, which was then 92 percent Black. Students from Evers, however, were not to be included in the Alternative Attendance Plan unless enrollment rose above 1,100 students (The enrollment during the 1966–67 school year was recorded as being 1,199.) An alternative plan was developed for its integration. This plan was to include the development of an enriched program at the school to be called the Program for Enriched Education in Lakeside (PEEL). The Lakeside Superintendent of Schools briefly described this program to the Board of Education in the following manner:

[The] Program for Enriched Education in Lakeside would involve integrated groups of youngsters in grades 4, 5, and 6, numbering 210. These children would be of high aptitude and interest, and the program would emphasize science, math, and a foreign language as well as a core program in the visual and performing arts to begin in September, 1967.

The planning for the PEEL Program was not done with any significant input from either the Black community that surrounds the school or the parents of poor Black students. Instead, educational "experts" were consulted in its development. This was believed by members of the Board of Education to give the program additional credibility and improve the image Evers presented to the city at large and to federal monitors:

> The superintendent of schools stated that, in the past three and one-half weeks, there had been two meetings with groups interested in the Quincy School [*Observer's comment*: Notice here that these "groups" are not specified to be community people.] and in making it a high-performing, exemplary learning center. He reported that commitments had been obtained from industry, Lakeside University, and others to furnish some of the special services needed to provide Quincy with the best program that could possibly be conceived. The intention, the superintendent indicated, is to give Quincy a new image and to make it accessible and acceptable to the community at large.

In order to pass on the decision to adopt the PEEL Program at this meeting, the Board waived its rule of tabling policy change items for one month before putting them to a vote. Protests were voiced by members of the audience. Mrs. Ida Goldfarb, chair of the Lakeside Committee for Integrated Education, was recognized:

> Mrs. Goldfarb requested that the Board of Education not vote on the Quincy Elementary School new curricular because there were so few people from the Quincy area present. Mrs. Goldfarb indicated a concern about the attitude of the Quincy area people and the fact that they were not present was evidence of their frustration.

Another member of the committee supported Mrs. Goldfarb's request:

> Mr. Ruppert requested that the Quincy proposal not be acted upon at this meeting. He stated that there had been a lack of Negro participation up to this point and to pass this item at this time would be a "trick" and the credibility gap would get worse.

At this point, the meeting was recessed for five minutes so that the Board could discuss the matter in private. One school board member made the following statement, upon reconvening: "What we have before us is a critical problem for the community of Lakeside. There has been leadership lacking in the area [the Quincy neighborhood] for a long time." The minutes of the meeting go on to report that this board member continued to discuss "the low graduation record of Negroes and their consequent inability to compete for employment and to improve their opportunities in life." He then moved the resolution to develop the new PEEL Program be tabled. This motion was seconded, but the president of the Board of Education "indicated that the tabling of this item did not necessarily mean that it would have to wait until the next regular meeting for final action." The PEEL Program was approved by the Board of Education, with no further input from the community, later that month.

In September 1967, the program was put into effect. The perspectives of Blacks and Whites concerning what is seen as the "progressive" period at Evers (1967–1972) are quite different. Many Whites with whom I spoke perceive the experiment as having been successful. White parents saw their children's school experience as "enriched" and "enlightening." They feel the program ended not because it failed, but because the administration at the school changed, and the attitude of "Black Power" turned the focus away from the needs of the White, middle-class children at the school to those of the poor, Black children and, in addition, because many of the children who had been in the program were moving on to junior high school.

Whites perceptions of an increased general militancy among Blacks in the city began to keep the next group of White children in their neighborhood schools, as well causing others in Evers to transfer out. These perceptions were based upon the rhetoric emerging from the Black community during the late 1960s and early 1970s. However, at no point in my investigation did I come across evidence of physical attacks by Blacks against White students during this period. There were no urban riots in Lakeside. Instead, physical violence in the community followed the pattern of disturbance characteristic of many urban Black ghettos, i.e., people committed violence against themselves and their neighbors.

Statements made by Black parents indicate that they feel the PEEL program may have benefited middle-class White children, but had a detrimental effect on poor, Black children at Evers, particularly those who were not academically prepared for the advanced curriculum:

> They was teaching kids French and our kids couldn't even read English. So what ended up happening was that you had a White school and a separate Black school in one building. A lot of kids got labeled as retarded in those days and were put in special classes 'cause they couldn't keep up with all those professors' and lawyers' kids.

Others were unhappy about the "open" atmosphere at the school, which they felt was at odds with the methods of discipline that many of the Black children were used to at home and in previous school experiences.

Tilly Post, the school district's community worker, expressed her feeling that there was a mismatch between the way teachers related to their students and what poor, Black children experienced in their homes. This was a concern voiced by many others as well:

> In the sixties permissive education came along and ruined Black children. Open classrooms are not for Black kids. They are not used to the permissiveness. Their homes are much more structured and they don't know how to handle the freedom. You can't say, "Now child, what would you like to do? Do your own thing!" Our kids aren't used to that and get lost.

Tilly felt that the mothers of poor, Black children are very restrictive with their children. Children are generally told what they can or cannot do, and the consequences of misbehavior often take the form of physical punishment.

The perspectives of all the Black parents with whom I spoke were consistent with that expressed by Tilly Post. They felt that their methods of discipline and control were firmer than those used by White, middle class parents. For example, Satticia Carpenter, a single Black mother in her forties, who is employed as a teacher aide in the Education Center, talked about what she perceived to be the differences between the ways White and Black parents relate to their children:

> Black parents don't talk to their kids the same way White folks do. If our kids don't bring the milk to the table or something like that, we don't say, "Dear, would you like to get the milk?" A Black mother would probably say, "Girl, get your ass off the chair and get that milk!"

Explorations of the socialization patterns of poor, urban Black families demonstrate that these child-rearing practices are not unique to Lakeside parents (Grier & Cobbs, 1968; Silverstein & Krate, 1975; Willie, 1970; Wortman, 1981). Silverstein and Krate (1975) describe the behavior they witnessed by poor Black mothers toward their children in schools, day-care centers and homes in central Harlem, and found that their observations were similar to others found in the literature. One such example of their observations relates to mothers of two-and three-year-old children, in the family rooms of Head Start centers while waiting for older children in classes nearby:

> Many of these mothers tried to restrain the children from using the toys in the room, left by the staff precisely for the children to play with. One mother, for example, held a rolled-up newspaper in her hand with which she would poke her little boy when he tried to move away from her and in the direction of the toys. Other mothers took a variety of actions that seemed designed to

repress movement, exploration, and vocalization in their young children. (p. 25)

The focus of lower-class socialization appears to be one of control over overt behavior. This emphasis was seen by Silverstein and Krate as related to the conditions of the lives of the mothers, which made this approach appear to be necessary for the well-being of their children. Grier and Cobbs (1968) see the punitiveness of the Black mother in our society as her means of protecting her children:

> She interprets the society to the children and takes as her task the shaping of their character to meet the world as she knows it. This is every mother's task. But the Black mother has a more ominous message for her child and feels more urgently the need to get the message across. The child must know that the white world is dangerous and that if he does not understand its rules it may kill him. (p. 51)

These points are significant, both to one's understanding of the failure of the more permissive approaches taken in the 1960s' experiments at Evers and in the development of more structured approaches in the years that followed. As illustrated in the following discussion, the perceived success of the latter type of approach is accounted for by the Evers staff in terms of its "fit" with the socialization patterns of Black families. What is not recognized, however, is that by further reinforcing these patterns, the culture of the Evers school may be continuing to teach Black children the submissiveness that was in the past perceived as necessary for survival. It is not preparing the Black child to succeed as an equal in the White world, where assertiveness and competitiveness are valued.

The 1970s

Teachers at Evers in 1981 related their highly structured teaching approach [*Distar*] and/or the use of firm discipline, including paddling, to their understanding of the socialization that their students have experienced outside of school. Their perceptions of the failure of the PEEL Program, and subsequent attempts at running the school as a whole from a permissive perspective in the early 1970s, were consistently presented as the rationale for the methods employed in the classroom today. The following statement, taken from an interview with Mary Flynn, a White second grade teacher who has been at Evers for nine years, presents a perspective that was shared by nearly all the teachers at Evers:

Mrs. Flynn: The school was huge when I came in, and pretty wild. Well, there was the PEEL program for gifted and talented children. Lots of open classrooms, some good things, but it was also a zoo. We had knifings in the halls. I came in at the end of that and things have changed a whole lot.

Question: Has your teaching style changed since you've been here?

Mrs. Flynn: A bit. I've always been very, very structured. Even back when I first started. Well, when I first came I was a new teacher too, so it's changed or I've developed a lot. But I've never been too big on open classrooms in this situation. But that's not to say that open classrooms wouldn't work in some other situations with some other kinds of kids.

The five years that followed the close of the PEEL experiment (1972–77) continued a good deal of its tradition in trying to create an environment that encouraged learning and put decision making in the hands of the students. The focus of the curriculum changed, however, to one that the new principal, Mr. Carp, a young Black man, considered to be more relevant to the lives of the children and their families. Changing the school's name to the Medgar Evers School was only a token as far as he was concerned. The PEEL Program had not, he believed, been consistent with the needs of the children and families from this neighborhood, either in its content or in the way it had been established. Instead, he set out to put in place a program based on participatory decision making by both staff and parents.

The following statement, issued in a memorandum to the school staff in 1973, introduced his plan to organize at Evers a program that would confront the "aspirations and technical survival requirements of the population served in this institution":

> The original motivation for change came during the era of federal mandates for balance in school populations; thus integration was our catalyst. At that time we based our philosophy upon the belief that importing high-achieving and highly academically motivated students in Evers would break the pattern of apathy toward academics that was exhibited by Black students. To believe this (*alone*) is dehumanizing and racist.

The new program focused on development of a "relevant" curriculum, including African and Afro-American history and culture and the "arts," i.e., music, poetry, theater, and visual arts.

Carla Jones, a Black woman in her late thirties, had been at Evers for 13 years in various paraprofessional roles, and in 1981 worked there as a "community aide." In this role, she focused on helping parents of Evers' students in a wide variety of ways, including negotiations with the Department of Social Services, household budgets, planning meals, and whatever other concrete assistance she had the time and resources to offer. Carla also communicated school concerns to those parents who were unwilling or unable to speak with other more "professional" members of the school's staff. She and others with a long history at the school believe that much of the turmoil during the 1970s was as related to continual program changes as it was to a lack of understanding of students' needs. As she put it, "I've been here 13 years. I've seen programs come and go and I've seen people come and go. If there's anything you want to know about the changes, just ask me."

Carla resents what was done to children, particularly during the late 1960s and early 1970s. She believes that this school was used as a proving ground for new theories on educating what were then known as "culturally deprived" children. She is especially angry at Mr. Carp, and feels that his approach was no better for the Evers child than were previous programs:

> He [Mr. Carp] was a middle class Black man pretending to be militant. He was afraid of the community here and never really was a part of it. He stopped all his Black Power jive when he saw it would get in the way of his career. He riled up a lot of folks and then backed down when the going got tough. He wasn't interested in educatin' our kids, just stirrin' folks up.

"Folks" were indeed "stirred up" by the mid-1970s, even in the relatively disorganized Black community surrounding the Evers school. By June 1977, Evers had exceeded its 1967 pre-PEEL percentage of Black enrollment of 92 percent. It was now 94 percent Black. Although the total enrollment of the school had decreased from almost 2,000 to approximately 600 students because of the city's Alternative Attendance Program, as well as declining school enrollments in general, Evers was, ten years after the city's first attempts to racially integrate its schools, still a segregated school.

In 1977, the Lakeside Board of Education was presented, for the second time, with a decree from the State Department of Education ordering that it integrate its schools. Several possible approaches were discussed at the June, 1977 Board of Education meeting. Unlike the meeting in 1967 this one was attended by many parents. The superintendent of schools was now a Black man, and a Black woman was one of the Board members. One plan that was discussed was the combining of Evers with the Frankfurt School, another predominantly Black school in an adjacent neighborhood, as well as with the Jefferson School, whose student body was 96 percent White.

Parents expressed their concern over the closing of another Black school. The city had already established a plan to close ten elementary schools as a way of dealing both with the disproportionate racial population of some of its schools, and the underutilization of facilities caused by declining school enrollments. Five of the elementary schools to be closed had Black populations that exceeded the overall percentage of Black elementary school students in the city, and three of these had populations that were over 50 percent Black.

The schools to be closed were chosen on the basis of age of the buildings, the use of their facilities, their racial composition and location. Having a high percentage of Blacks was not sufficient reason to close a school. It also had to be located in a neighborhood adjacent to one that was predominantly White. Then, hopefully, many of the children could walk to school, and "natural integration" would occur.

Because of the housing patterns that had developed in Lakeside as the result of urban renewal relocations, neither Evers nor Frankfurt elementary schools met these requirements. Although their populations were, respectively, 94 percent and 81 percent Black, both were "landlocked," i.e., they were centrally located within a neighborhood that was, by 1977, predominantly Black. Closing either school would have meant busing large numbers of Black children to other parts of the city. Furthermore, these children were predominantly poor and exhibited poor academic achievement, as evidenced by the low tested reading levels at both schools. Mr. Higgins, the Black principal at Frankfurt, spoke out strongly against the combining of these two schools at the June 1977 meeting:

> Mr. Higgins, principal at the Frankfurt School, explained that he did not feel that there was anything wrong with an all-Black school. He went on to say that the problems in most all-Black schools is that they are overwhelmed with kids with special problems, and that testing and test scores will not work out these special problems.
>
> "It is somewhat late in the game to place another problem on the Black community," said Mr. Higgins. "Will you please think about the Frankfurt students going out to Evers and Jefferson? We don't know how many teachers, administrators, aides, etc. will be added, but it is going to be very, very difficult. Right now, we have approximately 640 students at Frankfurt. And, as of yesterday, 602 problems—not just behavioral problems—had been referred to my office. We are only talking about 600 students, and now you are talking about 1000 with only two or three administrators. I cannot help but think of your sending all those kids, with all those special problems, to one brick building."

The motion to close Frankfurt was defeated. Members of the community were strongly opposed to closing Evers as well. Evers had come to be seen as the neighborhood school. Mr. Carp's campaign for community involvement and the increased level of Black self-awareness and pride on a national level, despite the cynical attitudes of some toward his motives, had helped create a group of parents who were very vocal about wanting Evers to remain open. Even though the voluntary transfer program would have allowed parents of Evers students to have transferred their children to any school in the city, many chose to have their children remain there. One mother expressed the reasons for sending her children to Evers in the following way:

> I send my kids here because it's close to home. I can run over to the school and get him if something should happen. I'm more comfortable with the staff. When your kid is bussed you don't know how they're treated. You know, the atmosphere at other schools is not as cheerful as here. I don't always trust what teachers say about my kid unless I know them awhile and here I can come over. Once my kid was sick and if he was at another school I couldn't get him. I got no cab fare or no car. The kids are more comfortable here. It's their school. Medgar Evers is Black. It's our school.

Mrs. Henty, a grandmother of two children at Evers and parent of children who went to school there in the 1960s, is also a neighborhood person who fought to keep Evers open. She was, however, disappointed with what she perceived to be happening there in 1981:

> Look, Evers is one of the strongest bases in this neighborhood. It probably is the only one right now and it's not doing too good as far as I can see. But the problems here are no different than if our kids were sent to the White man's school. The problem here is that the expectations for our kids are too low just as anywhere else. Whoever said that the only way a Black child could get educated was if he sat next to someone who is White? I never had anything to do with White folks all my life 'til I came up here. Never went to school with any of 'em and got a better education than our kids get up here. Evers is better for our kids 'cause it's in the neighborhood. They don't have to catch the yella cheese to the White man's school. They don't have to think that being with White folks is better than being with their own.

In September 1977, another solution to the problem of integrating Lakeside's schools was effected. Frankfurt was left open, and became a "magnet" school, offering advanced science and mathematics curricula to students throughout the city. The percentage of Black students at Frankfurt fell from 81 percent in 1976 to 53 percent in 1977 (Frankfurt had a 48 percent Black population in 1980). This change was the result both of the increase in the number of Whites attending the school and of a decrease in the number of its Black children. The actual number of Black students at Evers also fell dramatically because of the city's increased Alternative Attendance Program efforts that year.

Every parent of school-age children in the city received a brochure explaining the Alternative Attendance Program, which allowed any student to transfer to any school in the city. These brochures were still being sent to families in 1982. Evers remained the only school in the city into which a Black student from another "attendance area" could not transfer, and from which a White student might not transfer out. (A memorandum at the Pupil Services Office in the school district's downtown headquarters indicates that this regulation may be waived at parental request.) It is also important to note that special education students were exempt from this requirement because of their "special needs," which required special program consideration. It was this exemption that allowed Black students from predominantly White schools to be transferred to Evers after they have been identified as either emotionally disturbed or severely emotionally disturbed.

Another solution, also effected in 1977, to Evers' segregated status was a statistical one. Evers became paired with the disproportionately White Jefferson School, and became the "Evers–Jefferson Twin School." These two schools are still listed as one in the statistics concerning the Lakeside School District's student populations by race, which are sent to the state and federal governments. To make the union of these schools more than a marriage in name only, fifth and sixth graders switched schools for one month in the Spring of 1977. Later, in the Fall of 1977, third and fourth graders were added to the "Twin Project." This plan was unanimously perceived as a disaster. Children and teachers were in a state of confusion. Little school work was accomplished during "Twin Project" times. The plan was abandoned in the Fall of 1978. However, the school district's "racial census" continued to list the "Evers–Jefferson Twin School" as one school in 1980, and presented this nonexistent school as having a student body that is 42 percent Black. Neither Evers' nor Jefferson's population is listed separately in these data.

The "ethnic breakdown" of Evers' and Jefferson's student bodies' is listed separately in the school district's own records. This has not, however, been put together for public distribution in an easily read format, as have the "racial census" data cited above. The "ethnic breakdown" indicates that the kindergarten through sixth grade population of Jefferson during the 1979–80 school year was 70 percent White and 24 percent Black (the remaining population is distributed among Puerto Ricans, Orientals, Native Americans, and "others"). Evers is listed as having a 21 percent White population and a 76 percent Black population during the same year. The segregated nature of Evers' school-age population is still not truly represented by these numbers, which include 239 full-day kindergarteners in a total population of 454 students. If kindergarten students are not counted, Evers remains a 97 percent Black school.

This large number of kindergarten students at Evers (four times as many as the number in any other grade) represents the school district's latest attempt at integration. When the tandem idea failed, it was realized that another approach had to be taken. In the Fall of 1978, Evers became designated as an Early Education Center, and its fifth and sixth graders were sent permanently to Jefferson. This raised Jefferson's Black population. It also eliminated from Evers the older, more difficult to manage children with behavioral and academic problems. To further facilitate integration, Evers began to operate pre-kindergarten and full-day kindergarten programs. Admission to these programs was opened to anyone in the city, was free, and included bus transportation. It was and still is controlled by race, i.e., not more than 50% of the children in these programs can be Black. It was hoped that the White children who came to kindergarten at Evers would continue there once they reached first grade. This hope has not yet been realized.

At the same time as it became an Early Education Center, Evers became a "Total *Distar*" school. The *Distar* reading program had been introduced into the school in 1976 by Jean Smith, the school's instructional specialist. All instruction in reading, spelling, language, and math follows the *Distar* format. A highly structured, programmed approach to instruction, geared for low-income children, *Distar* directs its attention both to teaching skills in a step-by-step fashion and to teaching behaviors considered appropriate to the teaching-learning interaction. Reading is taught phonetically, sometimes using symbols other than letters. Often a specific section of the classroom is designated as the *Distar* corner, where eight to 12 chairs are arranged in a semicircular fashion, facing the teacher's chair in the center. Nothing is left to chance. The teacher has a script and is required to hold the book containing the day's lesson toward the children in a particular manner: point to the words, letters, numbers, pictures or other symbols in a pre-programmed sequence; and speak to the children following the language and rhythm described in the teacher's manuals and learned through extensive workshops.

Children are likewise expected to respond in the manner taught by the program. They recite during lessons only when recognized by the teacher, and then must respond following the pattern established as correct. For example, the teacher may hold up a day's lesson showing a picture of a boy riding on a horse. The goals of the language lesson may be to teach the answering of "who" and "what" questions and the use of prepositions. The teacher would begin by pointing to the picture of the boy and saying, "This is the boy. Get ready." Then, she would point to the group, nod her head, and they would recite in unison, as she snapped her finger to each word, "This—is—the—boy." One child might be picked to repeat the sentence. The teacher would then ask, "Who is this?", nod, point to the group; they would respond again, "This—is—the—boy," to the snap of her fingers. If one child answered, "The boy," instead of using the complete sentence, he or she might be asked to answer the question alone, or the teacher might say, "Someone didn't answer. Let's all try it again." Children are rewarded both by the immediate feedback given in each lesson, peer approval (or the avoidance of disapproval for holding back the group), and "points" for correct responses, which are converted into prizes. Workbooks are used in class and for homework for additional reinforcement. The children I observed seemed to learn the *Distar* routine quickly and enjoy its ritualistic quality. Teachers praised the carefully spelled-out lessons, and felt confident that they were "not leaving out anything." Even those individuals at Evers who disliked its rote, mechanized aspects favored its use. The reason given consistently for the adoption of *Distar* was that "It works for these kids." One second grade teacher expressed her feelings in the following way: "Most of these kids need this type of programmed approach because of the consistency and structure it offers." A special education teacher concurred, "Sure, it's repetitive, but that's what makes it good. I love it."

Evers: 1980–81

During the 1980–81 school year, the Medgar Evers' School had 454 students in kindergarten through the fourth grade, and ten prekindergarten classes with approximately 15 in each. Almost half of the kindergarten through fourth students, i.e., 239 children, were enrolled in either the kindergarten or "adjusted kindergarten" (a program for children who are of first-grade age chronologically, but who have been judged not ready for a first-grade classroom). The remaining students were in the first through fourth-grade program, which included an "alternative class" for students with learning and/or behavioral problems; one first-grade class; one first-second combination class for first-grade repeaters or slow second graders; one full second-grade class and one combination second-third grade class; one full third-grade class and a combination third-fourth grade class; and one full fourth-grade class. The average class size at Evers of 18 students was smaller than that found in most other elementary schools in Lakeside.

Three additional classes, each with eight students labeled as severely emotionally disturbed were also part of the school during the 1980–81 school year. From the Spring of 1977 until September 1981, two of these classes were housed in the older back section of the building, along with two other classes of older children (fifth and sixth graders) who had also been identified as severely emotionally disturbed. These four classes had, since 1977, been known collectively as the Education Center. In September

1980, additional fifth and sixth graders labeled as severely emotionally disturbed were no longer placed at Evers by the school district's Committee on the Handicapped. The two classrooms remaining in the Education Center were then placed in the main wing of the school and were publically identified as Mr. Pallard's and Mrs. Sheppard's classes. The Ever's staff, however, more often than not continued to refer to these classes as the Education Center. The third class for children identified as severely emotionally disturbed placed at Evers that year was distinguished from the other two and was referred to as the Withdrawn S.E.D. class. This distinction was made because the students in this classroom did not display the disruptive behavior that was characteristic of children who had been previously placed in the Education Center. Rather, these students were nonverbal or had poor language skills, were not socially interactive, and were significantly developmentally delayed.

Of the 12 full-time classroom teachers at Evers, eight are White females; four are Black, three females and male. The support personnel at the school include an instructional specialist, helping physical education teacher, art teacher, music teacher, librarian, instrumental music teacher, Title I reading teacher, social worker, psychologist, school nurse, and resource teacher. All are White, except for the male social worker and the female music teacher. Five of the six-man custodial staff are White. The cafeteria workers are all women, the majority Black. The paraprofessionals (teaching assistants, community aide, and CETA aide) are all Black women. The principal's secretary is a White woman in her fifties who has been at Evers since the mid-1960s. The current principal, Mrs. Rivers, is a Black woman, as have been the two principals immediately preceding her. The average age of staff members is in the mid-thirties. Teachers and most of the staff members have been at Evers for an average of ten years.

Mrs. Rivers had been a teacher at Evers during the late 1960s and early 1970s. She characterizes the typical Evers teacher as one of "a unique breed of individual. These teachers know how to take care of things. If I wanted, I could make this the easiest job in the world. Just sit back and watch things run themselves. These teachers know how to be problem solvers." That the teachers have run the show here for the past 15 years is not a surprise, given that there have been five principals during that time, while most of the teachers have stayed. Certainly Mr. Carp's policy of participatory decision making helped, but the lack of consistent or continual leadership for this staff has pushed teachers into a position where they have had to make decisions on their own.

The ten years between 1969 and 1979 were characterized by the staff as a period of turmoil and change that led to the development of the program and approaches taken in 1981. Teachers' attitudes toward their students had often been shaped by past negative interactions with students and their parents. In formal interviews and informal conversation, staff members often cited past failures as the reasons for present approaches. There existed a tendency among Evers' teachers to expect that their students would not be able to function effectively in school without strict rules and regulations guiding and controlling these children's social behavior.

My observations of children in several classrooms at different grade levels, at different times of the day, and during different periods of the year presented an impression of groups that were very well behaved. This was the case not only when children were under the direct supervision of their teacher, but also when they were left on their own, either when their teacher spoke with me or when they had finished their "seat work" and chose activities for "free play." Teachers consistently related their perception that the children are well behaved because of the structure in their rooms, without which, they feel, their students would be lost. And yet, I observed many of these children as able to monitor their own behavior, in and out of the classroom, even when their routine was disturbed and no external structure was apparent.

The following passage, taken from field notes recorded during my observation of Mary Flynn's second-grade class, is typical of behavior I observed in a variety of situations and in regular education classrooms. It demonstrates that although some of the children have difficulty in functioning on their own, many are quite capable of doing so:

Group 2 now goes with the teacher to the *Distar* corner. They sit in a semicircle facing the teacher. She opens the book to a page that has a word printed on it. The first letter is in red. She points to the letter and says, "What sound?" with stress on the word "sound." Some of the children don't respond, and so she repeats the clue. "What sound?" They respond in unison. She then says, "Get ready: what word?" and runs her finger under the entire word. They respond in unison.

I look over at Carl's (the mainstreamed child) group and he is now working. The little girl who has been daydreaming is still doing so. Another little girl on his other side has her hair done in neat little rows of braids, each braid held in place by a plastic barrette of a different color and shape. She is sucking on her fingers and looking around. Mary's reading group is interrupted by a boy who comes into the room, goes up to her and hands her a note. He is late because he has been to the nurse, he says. He goes to his seat in Group 1 and takes out his folder. A little girl now comes up to the teacher. She has just lost her tooth. "Congratulations, that's wonderful," responds Mary. She takes the tooth and the girl to the sink in the corner of the room, suggests that the girl rinse her mouth, and then wraps the tooth in a tissue and tells the girl to take it with her. Another teacher comes into the room and calls out, "Mrs. Flynn, can I borrow some paste?" Mary gets up, goes over to a shelf and hands the teacher a jar of paste. The other woman asks, "Do you have a lot of kids out, too?" Mary says that she has six out. The teacher thanks her and leaves. The children have either been working or watching the two women. Several of the kids remark about how tall and thin she is after she leaves. Mary responds, "She sure is thin. I wish I was as thin." [*Observer's Comments*: The other woman had a model-like figure and was wearing faded designer jeans, which accentuate that look. Mary is a thin woman herself, and today, as usual, is casually dressed in cotton slacks, a blouse and flat-heeled sandals.]

Mary returns to her *Distar* group, which has been waiting patiently. She picks up just where she left off: "What word?" The group responds in unison. I glance over at Carl and see that he is now working steadily.

Mary, the teacher of the second-grade classroom described above, is a White woman who has been teaching at Evers for nine years, and has taught several different grade levels. She feels that in a setting in which the majority of children come from "deprived" backgrounds, and "because they lack many of the social and academic skills necessary for success in the public schools, a highly structured approach is necessary."

Sally Brown, a fourth grade teacher who has been at Evers for more than ten years, echoed Mary's sentiments. She is a Black woman in her early thirties and was in the last months of her pregnancy when I observed her classroom. She expressed her understanding of the need for discipline in the following statement:

> Kids have got to learn discipline. It's like I tell them, when they leave here and go out into those other schools, those teachers are not going to put up with any nonsense. So I want these kids to learn that now. . . . I have five girls and 19 boys in my class. I guess it's because I'm stricter than the other fourth grade teacher and so they give me the hardest kids to handle. I don't believe that kids should be up and out of their seats and wandering around the room. They have to have discipline, be in their seats and concentrating in order to learn anything. I want them to grow up to be men who can take care of themselves and their families. I met a kid the other day. He was a kid I used to know over here. He's about 16 years old and he's on the street already, with nothing to do. I don't want these kids to end up that way. Other schools will just throw them out, so I give them the discipline here so that they can make it. I'm hard on them, I know, but I never say anything to them that I don't mean, and they know ahead of time what I'll do if they get out of line.

Observation in both these classrooms proved that these women act on their beliefs. Their styles are very different, however. Mary is softer in her approach and uses a good deal of positive verbal reinforcement. Her classroom is full of interesting materials and art work, as well as displays of the children's work. The seating arrangements for the children consist of three clusters of tables and chairs. Each cluster reflects a *Distar* group. The arrangement encourages the children to interact but only with children in their group. During work time, the children must work silently at their seats. The morning's work is spelled out carefully to the children each day, and so it is highly predictable. The children can earn points and win a prize after the accumulation of a specified number of points. My overall impression of this classroom was that it was one that the children enjoyed. Most of the students completed their work in a relaxed and interested manner. If a child was having difficulty, Mary was available to help, provided that the child asked for help in the "proper" way.

There were a great many distractions in the flow of the school day. In addition to my frequent visits, which the children acknowledged with friendly smiles from their seats, other teachers and staff were continually coming into the room. Kids were going in and out of the class to go to the nurse's office for cut fingers, bloody noses, etc. None of these events seemed to disturb the smooth flow of the room. Mary remained soft-spoken and attentive to the children through it all. Carl Smith, the special education student mainstreamed in this class, was an integral part of the room. It would be impossible to identify him as handicapped in this setting.

Sally Brown's style of discipline and structure was quite different from Mary's, and often disturbing to my White, middle class sensibilities. As in Mary Flynn's second-grade classroom, the morning's work was spelled out carefully and the children knew exactly what was expected of them each day. The rules for proper behavior are well known, i.e., stay in your seat and complete your own work silently. However, unlike Mary, Sally is often hard in her tone and shows a minimal degree of flexibility toward the children and any difficulty they may express regarding their work. She would yell, "Shut up and sit down!" at any child out of his or her seat. If, for example, one child was helping another, Mrs. Brown would call out to that child, "You shut up, sit down and get into your own seat, chile! If she don't know what to do, that's her problem and not yours."

Sally's approach can be best summarized as "no nonsense," and is symbolized by the physical environment of the classroom. The desks are in traditional rows, facing the front blackboard and the teacher's desk. There is no art work in the room. The day's assignments are written on the chalkboard, as are two short lists of names under the headings "No List" and "100 Club." These lists represent a type of behavior modification approach used with the students. Being on the No List means losing privileges, while the 100 Club means a reward. The child mainstreamed from the Education Center, in this class, stood out from the others in the room only because he was the only White child and because he arrived late in the morning, staying only for one hour, to complete his reading assignment.

Both these women see their role as one of surrogate-mother for many of their students. Mary approaches this role by being very nurturing and showing concern over the children's physical as well as intellectual and emotional well-being. Sally, with all her harshness and apparent inflexibility, likewise sees herself and is seen by many of the children as a mother-figure. One of the most striking ways that this is manifested is in her contact with each of the children's families. Whereas Mary only contacts families when there is a problem or on appointed conference days, Sally visits every home at the beginning of each year and continues to do so throughout the school year. Sally describes the importance of these visits thusly:

> I go to every kid's house and visit with their families. They really like that and it helps me to get to know the kids. They know that I'm in the neighborhood and can stop in any time. Some of the families are real good and you can see it in the kids. These kids like me to see their parents too and the kids that are having problems don't feel like I'm just picking on them. . . . You know when I can't figure out what's happening with a kid, when everything that I try here doesn't work, I'll go to the house again and it doesn't take me long to know what the problem is. I just go there, spend some time, look around, and there it is, as clear as can be and I understand why this kid is having problems.

The disciplinary techniques used by both Sally and Mary were identical: losing privileges, staying after school, writing 100 times "I must not . . . ," or paddling. Paddling is viewed as a tactic of last resort, and is used by all the teachers at Evers. The reason most often given for using this type of punishment was that the teacher had tried "everything else" and was worn out. Occasionally a child was paddled if the teacher wanted to scare the offending child and/or the whole class. This form of punishment was seen as an approach "these kids" could relate to, since it was what they were used to receiving at home. Paddling was done either in front of the class, with the child bending forward and being swatted on the bottom several times with a flat wooden paddle, or in the principal's office, with the principal serving either as "executioner" or observer. Mrs. Rivers, the new principal in the 1980–81 school year, was opposed to paddling and recognized that it had become an institutionalized method of punishment at Evers that would be difficult to eliminate.

Mrs. Rivers: Kids have been sent down here and start to cry before I even say anything. They're afraid I'm going to paddle them. I say to them, "I'm not here to paddle you." Maybe I've lost some power because of it; I don't know. I want to find out what the problem is. I will do something. There will be other consequences. When I was an administrative assistant here before, I did paddle and it did solve the problem instantly, for a brief time. But then I realized that the problem didn't really go away. At the other school as principal I worked with parents very closely and I began to realize that parents do very little spanking of their children and so it doesn't have the meaning to them you might like it to have.

Question: But many people here have said that they felt that the parents of many of the children here do use physical means to discipline their kids, and that's why they used paddling.

Mrs. Rivers: But that's contradicting yourself. It's kind of backwards. They're not saying it works and we'll do it too. But the one thing that they haven't found out from parents is that it doesn't work. People usually spank out of pure frustration. They don't know what else to do. I knew a kid who got some broken blood vessels in his fanny. I witnessed the paddling and it wasn't bad, but some kids are very sensitive. So why take the chance of hurting the child? Philosophically, I don't believe in it, and physically, I think it's bad.

Question: Are the teachers aware of how you feel about this?

Mrs. Rivers: There are a few that I have spoken to directly, but I have not made a general announcement to the faculty about it. Because there are some teachers who feel strongly about it and believe in it and I feel that they would never send a kid to me if they knew I would not be paddling the child. I'll do other things.

Mrs. Flynn's and Mrs. Brown's classrooms were typical of the other classrooms in several respects. In addition to these teachers' perspectives regarding the need for structure and the carefully spelled-out "rules" that were visibly displayed in every room I visited, each room had its *Distar* corner or section. One classroom even had a large bulletin board display that read "We Love *Distar*," beneath which hung samples of students' "perfect papers." Each room also had a television set, which was occasionally tuned in to "Sesame Street." The television was sometimes used in the mornings as the children filed into the room after their breakfast in the cafeteria, and before the "opening exercises" which came into every classroom, office, and hallway through the public address system, connecting each room and individual in the school with one another.

There were aspects of the classrooms at Evers that made them appear quite different from others I have visited elsewhere. The most obvious is the racial composition of the students. In every classroom there were no more than one or two White children. These children appeared to be, in most cases, the most poorly dressed and groomed in the room, and were often in the lowest *Distar* groups. Most classrooms lacked evidence of ongoing projects in science or social studies, except for the schoolwide project on "famous Black Americans," which lasted for the entire month of February. In classrooms where science projects were displayed, the same ones remained on display for many months. Extra reading materials, such as children's story books and encyclopedias, were either absent altogether or minimal. Little creative art work or materials was displayed. Mary

Flynn's classroom was unique in its continually changing decor of posters, mobiles and paintings.

One characteristic of the classrooms that came to symbolize the current Evers approach toward education was its windows, which, I mentioned earlier, were translucent plastic, covered with heavy wire mesh. Thus, some light was let into the rooms, but the children could not see out. They were therefore not distracted by the reality of the world outside their classroom windows. The use of *Distar* as a schoolwide approach to the teaching of language arts skills, along with some of the disciplinary practices used, can be seen to serve the same purposes as do the translucent windows seen in every classroom: they limit the children's experiences so that they may behave appropriately *now*. The children are learning the "basics," and their behavior is controlled, but the development of creative processes that involve inferential thought and independent problem solving skills needed for later, higher level academic tasks, is being limited, both by the continual reinforcement of rote learning and by the lack of time spent on other, more creative activities or problem solving. Most of the staff members who have been at Evers over the past decade feel that this is a sacrifice that must be made in order to teach basic skills to "these kids."

Since the introduction of the *Distar* reading program in 1976, the reading skills of Evers students have improved overall, seeming, initially, to vindicate the *Distar* approach. However, they begin to decline when the students reach the fourth grade and inferential thinking, as well as content, become important. Preliminary evidence of this decline can be seen in Table 4.1, which summarizes the reading levels at Lakeside's elementary schools during the 1979–80 school year, as measured by the California Achievement Test (C.A.T.), and compares them to Evers' and to national norms.

The fact that the average tested reading levels of second and third-grade students at Evers conforms to the national norm demonstrates that there were many children there whose true achievement was at an above-average level. As Mercer (1973) has demonstrated, children who come to "Anglo-Dominant" schools from socio cultural backgrounds that differ from the dominant culture are at a decided disadvantage when they are asked to perform on standardized measures of achievement. They therefore are

TABLE 4.1
Reading Levels at Evers, 1979-1980

	Grade 2	Grade 3	Grade 4
Evers	2.7	3.7	3.3
Total City	3.2	4.3	5.1
National Norm	2.7	3.7	4.7

seen to score lower than their "true" ability, because of both the content of the assessment device and the processes that are demanded (which include inferential thinking and problem-solving skills, particularly in the higher elementary grades). This may, in part, explain the poor performance of Evers fourth graders on the C.A.T. Certainly, additional explanations include a decline in student motivation for school acheivement and the cumulative effects of poverty on these children.

By gearing its programs for the average child at Evers (which is a child functioning below the level of the average Lakeside child), Evers is doing precisely what most other schools in the American educational system have done, i.e., aim instruction at the middle-range students. There are many opportunities for the child who falls below the Evers norm to receive the help he or she may need—Title I reading teacher, Resource Room assistance, the Alternative Class, after-school tutorial program, combination grade-level classrooms, and cross-grade placement in the most appropriate *Distar* group. However, the above-average child has no opportunity at Evers for enriched programming or instruction that would stretch his creative abilities and cognitive skills.

Greg Parnell, an experienced teacher in his first year at Evers, is a Black man who grew up in Lakeside. His family migrated here from the South in the 1950s. Unlike the other teachers at the school, Greg brought my attention to the three students in his second- and third-grade combination class that had done better than average on the achievement tests given in 1980, one second grader scoring at a 3.8 grade level in mathematics. Although these students were the exceptions in Greg's class, their significance lies in his focus on them during our interview, rather than on those who are far below the norm, as was the case with the other teachers with whom I spoke. No other teacher mentioned the problem of advanced students being held back, although in every class I visited, there was a small group of two or three who flew through their *Distar* workbooks and then quietly amused themselves with coloring books or one of the few puzzles in the classroom, while the teacher attended to the slower children.

Although familiar with Evers and its history, Greg has not been socialized by the experiences here during the past few years, as have the majority of Evers' teachers. He recognized that many of his students had a good deal more academic potential than that which was called upon by the *Distar* programs. In the following discussion, he related his belief that the problem his students faced with their school work was not their intellectual ability, but their ability to make decisions and to apply problem-solving approaches from one situation to another.

> One reason that many of these kids did so poorly on these tests is that they have difficulty in following verbal directions. But that was at the beginning of

the year and they're better now because we work on it. And some of them have a big problem in that they don't think that they know how to follow directions. It's not that they don't know; they refuse to. They'd rather ask somebody than try to do it on their own. Now like we'll do math games and stuff like that and I'll demonstrate, particularly in the lower group, the first page. Now the second page may be just a little different, like they'll put a graph, but you're still doing the same math but it looks different. I show them how they explain it all right on the top of the page. They just don't do it, but will come to me with, "Mr. P., how do I do it?" So I'll say, "Did you read the top of the page?" And they'll say, "No." I think it's just a matter of their being told so much of the time what to do. I want these kids to be able to follow directions before they go and ask somebody else to be giving them something. There's an awful lot being given to these kids. Most of these kids are poor and all their life everything is given to them. And they will grow up looking for people to be giving them something. . . . There's nothing in *Distar* like a regular writing lesson, where the kids get a chance to write on their own, and that needs to happen. I do like it [*Distar*] with some kids. But with some of my kids it's not worth it. Because they could be doing so much and it holds them back.

June Rivers, Evers' principal, is a Black woman who is a "seventh-generation Lakesider." Like Greg, she had not been at Evers during its most recent turbulent period. She had taught at Evers for seven years before "taking the plunge," as she puts it, "into the real world." She left Evers at the time Mr. Carp became principal, and "things were beginning to fall apart." Mrs. Rivers became a social studies supervisor for the city, and then became principal at another, more racially balanced and traditional elementary school, where she had been for the past three years. She talked about the changes that have occurred at Evers and the problems it now faces:

People are not expecting enough of our kids here. Prior to 1971 and for a time after that, the feeling at Evers was that kids needed to develop coping skills and these skills were seen as separate from academic skills. Well, since then that has changed and academic skills have taken precedence, sometimes leaving out coping skills and sometimes trying to incorporate them too. The teaching of creativity has fallen by the wayside and "basics" have taken over. In a lot of ways this has been a reaction to the way things were done before when there were many creative programs but the kids really didn't learn much in terms of skills. . . . If I was to suggest a Gifted Program for Evers, people would laugh at me. . . . We need to teach kids to cope by teaching them the meaning of the language used out there. For example, the other day a kid was sent to me for fighting and I used the word "intimidate." He had no idea what that meant, but he sure knew how to do it. Something like teaching kids the proper ways to dress and the meanings of words and how to use them are very important, not as in the past, where the attitude was, "Well, they'll pick it up." If these kids don't pick this stuff up here, they'll never pick it up anywhere.

During her first year as principal at Evers (1980), Mrs. Rivers helped set up a Parent Room in the multipurpose room, a double-sized classroom on the first floor, next to her office. Tilly Post, the community worker, and Carla Jones, the community aide, have been working with the Parent Teacher Organization, getting parents involved in planning the physical layout of the room as well as its purposes. Teachers have not become involved. Instead, a handful of mothers have gotten furniture and a refrigerator donated and have begun to plan the Parent Room program. Sewing classes were the first thing organized. Tilly's hope is that mothers who are now sitting at home in Middle Village will come across the street to the school, talk with other mothers, possibly learn a skill that may make their lives more pleasant, and, at the same time, become involved in their children's education. This involvement will hopefully facilitate a better fit between the child's life at school and at home. Currently, this match is being accomplished by focusing on the overt control of children's behavior, using practices teachers believe parents use at home.

The lack of teacher involvement in the Parent Room demonstrates a significant change in the role of the teacher at Evers from what it had been in the late 1960s and early 1970s. In those days, teachers were required to make home visits. Today, only a few teachers go to their students' homes. The school's social worker, community worker, or community aide does the visiting. Teachers, for the most part, don't believe that this is part of their job, and some expressed fear of going into the housing projects or walking in the neighborhood. Past experiences and subjective interpretations of student and parental behavior replaced direct contact with the child's life outside of school as the basis for the assumptions teachers make regarding their students' needs.

There was a general assumption at Evers that no one at home paid attention to "these kids'" emotional needs. The fact that many of the children lived in single-parent families or with their "grands" was offered as evidence. This assumption had a significant effect on teachers' interactions with their students. They believed that their students were "unloved." Their role, therefore, needed to include nurturing children's emotional needs. This belief tempered their "Distaresque" approach.

Throughout the school, a genuine concern and caring for children's emotional and physical well-being was evident. For example, in the Winter months, the large lobby inside the double glass-door entrance was used as a gathering place for the children and their teachers. Mrs. Rivers would often leave her office to greet the children. She and others demonstrated a good deal of concern over the children's outer clothing. Most of the children were warmly dressed, but any child lacking outer clothing would go home at the end of the day with the gloves, hat, boots or jacket he or she might need. It was not unusual to see a teacher sitting and talking over a problem with a student. Noses were blown, and bottoms paddled, just as the children's mothers would or should be doing at home. The warmth exhibited by teachers toward their students, coupled with swift discipline, matched the most obvious aspects of child-rearing practices in poor, Black families often described in the literature (Grier & Cobbs, 1968; Jeffers, 1967; Silverstein & Krate, 1975; Willie, 1970; Wortman, 1981).

· Evers has been referred to by many of the people with whom I spoke as a "family." Teachers often see themselves as surrogate mothers to the children in their classrooms. But, the sense of "family" more often referred to the staff's feelings about the relationships they had with one another and their mutual understanding about the needs of their students and their families. Many were distrustful of me and soon became defensive about my questioning of *Distar*. One woman suggested to the principal that I was a spy sent to discredit the program.

I came to see that the mutual understandings that have developed among the majority of the staff at Evers have enabled them to integrate children into their classrooms who, in other settings in this city, were seen as markedly deviant. They perceived all of their students to be in need of emotional and academic support. They assumed that "these kids," i.e., average Evers students, if left without clearly defined limits and rules, would go "off the wall" and create the "zoo" they recall this school as having been in 1971.

All the teachers felt that they have always been working with students who are emotionally disturbed. Each class already was accommodating students who have been identified and labeled as emotionally disturbed as part of their regular enrollment. These students received special assistance in the Resource Room for part of their day. As long as these labeled children could fit into the program they had developed for their regular students, who were also perceived as emotionally needy, teachers were willing to include a small number of those who had been labeled as severely emotionally disturbed into their classrooms as well. As the development of the Education Center is traced in the following chapter, it is important to keep in mind that the perspectives of Evers' teachers regarding their role were often not shared by teachers in other Lakeside schools.

5

The Education Center

The History of the Education Center

In 1968, the Community Action Agency (C.A.A.) was established in the city of Lakeside with federal funds. Like similar agencies established throughout the country, the C.A.A. had the goal of establishing and administering programs in the community that would, in their respective neighborhoods, meet the needs of the people who fell within the poverty guidelines established by the federal government. One problem such agencies hoped to address was the education of Black children. The low number of Black students graduating from Lakeside schools in 1968, compared to their numbers in lower grades, indicated that public school programs were not successfully reaching Black children. Tutorial programs were therefore set up at seven youth centers in the city.

The C.A.A. became aware that its tutorials were not enough to meet the needs of many Black students. These children were seen as being basically unserved by the public school system. Peter Stein, the original director of the Education Center, described "unserved" children in the following way:

> They may not have been in school or were getting minimal services or inadequate services in school. . . . well, if they're not in school they'll probably be in the courts or be suspended or be put in special education programs that were like basement programs, watered-down programs. You have to realize that these were pre- 94–142 days. In addition, what was happening was that the community was just getting sensitive to the fact that a disproportionate number of kids who were minorities were being put in watered-down programs. . . . Yes, so the complaint was that a lot of our kids were being suspended, sent home, dropping out, being pushed out of school, whatever.

This increased awareness occurred at the same time that it had become apparent that the PEEL experiment at Evers was not meeting the academic and social needs of many of the Black students from the immediate neighborhood surrounding Evers. By 1972 that program had ended, and Mr. Carp had become principal. His focus on a "relevant" curriculum, student

69

participation in decision making, and political activism had increased Black parent and student awareness of the social and political issues that were being reflected in the educational system. Unfortunately, his educational approach did not meet the needs or level of readiness of many Evers students. As a result, many children remained unserved.

The C.A.A. felt they needed to develop a more comprehensive program, and so, when Peter Stein submitted a program description to them that included the use of "behavioral technology" and community resources in an "innovative package," they forwarded it to Washington. His proposal was accepted, and he was later hired as program director. Stein, a young White man who had recently arrived in Lakeside, had no experience working in education, nor any knowledge of the city, its politics, or its educational system. Stein believed that because he was an unknown in city politics, the forces that he perceived to be at odds with one another were unable to identify him as an agent of any of the other special interest groups. He identified these political forces as the board of directors that oversaw all activities of the C.A.A., the C.A.A. program directors, and the Lakeside School District.

The board of directors consisted predominantly of elected officials who were supposed to be representatives of the local communities. These communities were, however, political sectors, none of which fully represented the large geographic tract in which most of the Black population lived at that time. A mayoral appointee and people from the private sector were also represented on the board. Approval of the board of directors was necessary for the implementation of the program. They approved the project with the stipulation that it had to operate under a cooperative contract with the school district. Stein agreed.

Stein was unaware that his agreement with the board of directors would be viewed as treason by the C.A.A. program directors, but a friend soon explained to him the implications of the situation he had created:

> Well, he told me that what I had done was crazy and that they had basically put me on a no-win mission because the school district and the C.A.A. had been at war for years. C.A.A. was now representing the voice of the people who feel they have been excluded for a long time and they are going to literally think that you are either too naive or purposely getting them involved in an endeavor with their critics sitting right inside. They'll all laugh in your face.

The C.A.A. doubted that the school district would consider a cooperative contract, but Stein went ahead and spoke with the superintendent of schools. The school district agreed to the program, with the stipulation that the children to be sent to the program would be those identified by the district psychiatrist, Dr. Flagg. Stein put it this way:

He would know the kids who aren't getting services. I set up a committee consisting of the psychiatrist and some people who were social workers in the school. The kids got to the psychiatrist's office from the school social workers. The route was basically the school social workers would feed it to him, if he'd seen the kid, fine; if he hadn't, then he would go see the kid. If he said thumbs up, then he called me and said why don't we go look at this kid in such and such a school.

The first five children in the program were described as "extremely aggressive" boys, Black, between the ages of nine and 11 years old. Two of the boys lived in foster homes, two with single mothers, and one in a two-parent family. All were poor. In 1972, these boys were not identified as severely emotionally disturbed, but rather were designated as Lakeside Academic Rehabilitation (L.A.R.) students, and their program identified as the Education Center. It was not until 1977, the year that the program was moved to Evers and fell totally under the jurisdiction of the city school district, that the label "severely emotionally disturbed" was applied to these students.

By establishing the school district's psychiatrist as the person responsible for identifying that students would attend the Education Center, the Lakeside school system created a precedent which determined which of its students would later become identified as emotionally disturbed. Although the children attending the Education Center in its early years were not officially labeled in this way, the program was operated with the understanding that these students were indeed deviant and in need of clinical intervention. The selection of students and the programs developed in the Education Center followed the psychiatrist's theoretical and personal understanding. This definition of children's behavior would later intersect with the social and political events occurring in Lakeside during the 1970s.

Dr. Flagg feels that the children he referred to the original Education Center are the same kinds of children that he today labels Severely Emotionally Disturbed. Both sets of children, he believes, exhibit the same set of behavior "patterns." I asked him why he thought this group of children were primarily Black and male. I recorded Dr. Flagg's response in note form as he spoke:

Well, I'm really glad you asked that question because I really feel strongly about that. There are three major things that attribute to the fact that you have more Black kids who are emotionally disturbed. The first is that you have a higher percentage of broken homes. Now it's a universal problem. Lots of kids from broken homes. But, in the Black family, it means an inconsistent, haphazard house, okay? Now remember, you are hearing this from a psychiatrist.

The second part is cultural and it has to do with Black women raising kids in a discriminatory way. By discriminatory, I mean in a way that discriminates against the sex of your child. You know you have this mama and she'll have three or four kids and the boys, well, she just wants to get rid of the boys as soon as she can. She'll send them out in the streets: "Leave me alone boy!" The girls will stay home in the house and she'll want to keep the girls next to her and help around the house, wash the dishes, wash the floor, and this way the girls can form a strong identification with her. But the orientation with the boy is, "Get him out." They are no good, you know. . . .

That comes from the fact that he's just like the Black daddy, if she knows who the Black daddy is. You know, what does the Black daddy do? He does nothing around the house. He comes and he goes. He usually doesn't work. He's hanging around on the street, living off her money. . . .She puts up with it because, you know what they say: "A little piece of a man is better than no man at all." You know, Black men are studs, that's what they are. It's sort of like you could look at the Black family like a dairy farm. You know what they do with bull calves, they send them out to be veal. That's what these women do to their Black boys. Their attitude is, "You ain't fit for learning." Most of the men are Black male prostitutes, they are pimps. They have been raised in that way and in that tradition. They are bulls. It's slavery, that's what the Black man was. They have been written off by their mothers. And when a boy is born, you know what she says: "My God, another boy!" And most of them as a result feel this inadequacy from that.

They [emotionally disturbed children] are the product of this culture that I'm talking about. You know I dumped dozens of them on Peter Stein years ago, and these kids all had this pattern.

Dr. Flagg's position clearly reflects the notion of a "culture of poverty" that dominated the social science literature during the middle and late 1960s (Baratz & Baratz, 1973; Moynihan, 1965; Riessman, 1962; Valentine, 1968). In fact, he seems to be echoing the "tangle of pathology" described in the widely publicized "Moynihan report":

At the heart of the deterioration of the fabric of Negro society is the deterioration of the Negro family. It is the fundamental source of weakness of the Negro community at the present time. . . . Unless this damage is repaired, all the effort to end discrimination and poverty and injustice will come to little. (Moynihan, 1965, p. 5)

Extensive media coverage of this document may, in fact, have conveyed to both professionals and to the public a point of view that explained the problems of Blacks from a "blaming the victim" perspective (Ryan, 1971). The Black family most certainly was, and still is, faced with enormous problems. However, explaining the cause of the problems faced by Black male children as the exclusive responsibility of their mothers ignores the social conditions that are responsible for the instability of the two-parent Black family. In addition, defining the normal family as a two-parent, nuclear unit predisposes clinicians to see the Black children raised in single-parent families as pathological. This definition may ignore the strengths seen in many of these families. The social networks, for example, that are an integral part of the Black family, are often ignored.

> Black families have developed social networks consisting of kin or "non-kin they regard as kin" for the purpose of sharing limited resources and services as well provide daily support. In most instances, female-headed single-parent households are a part of one of these "domestic networks." . . . chronic unemployment/underemployment combined with a welfare system that rewards fatherless homes has forced the kin system to discourage the development of stable conjugal unions. Stated in another fashion, the welfare system/dual labor market engenders survival strategies based upon single-parent households while discouraging (1) social mobility, and (2) intact nuclear households. (Cross, 1979, p. 3).

Dr. Flagg's interpretations rest on a stereotypical view of Blacks that results in ethnocentric (White) definitions of children's behavior. The "scientific" explanations he offers explain the behavior of low-income Black children in terms of their "illness." The interventions that follow proceed on the assumption that changing the child's responses to ones considered "appropriate" will best serve the needs of the child. Interventions aimed at supporting parents or facilitating changes in the community are not considered.

It is apparent that more than the child's needs were served by establishing the Education Center. The city school district certainly stood to gain by supporting the program in its early years, if only because of the image of cooperation this support presented to the community during a time of frustration and militant rhetoric. Racial integration attempts had not been successful, and Blacks locally as well as nationally were turning toward "self-determination" and "community control" of social programs. The establishment of an educational program within the community, operated outside of a public school setting, allowed the C.A.A. to have the sense of control it had sought, while it also released the school district from responsibility for some of its most troublesome students.

The original Education Center program was housed in an office building in the downtown section of the city. This space was paid for by the federal grant the C.A.A. had received, and allowed for programming that Peter Stein feels would have been impossible to provide within the confines of a public school building. Although the first teachers hired by the school system were, according to Stein, "vets with emotionally disturbed kids," they were not trained in the type of behavior modification approaches he felt to be necessary. The two original teachers were fired, and Stein, with the help of "instructional technologists" from Lakeside University, hired and trained a new staff.

By the end of the first year, there were 30 students, three teachers, three teacher assistants, and an administrator (Stein) in the program. Of these students, 22 were boys, two-thirds of whom were Black. There were also eight Black girls in the program. The 30 children were described by Stein in the following way:

> They were very aggressive, impulsive street kids who were easily provoked to a lot of fighting, a lot of testing behaviors, a lot of tantrums. They did not respond with any adults, were very rebellious, were very well programmed. The minute an adult told them anything, they'd say, "Go fuck off!" or storm off.

The program established for these students focused on reacclimating them toward academic tasks. This was done by the use of behavioral strategies ("token economy," individual contracting, and "time-out" procedures), crisis management, and attempts to establish "meaningful relationships" with the students and their families. According to Stein:

> We would use a token economy and a lot of individual contracting and a lot of individual crisis work. A lot of basically confronting passive behaviors. We had a room right off from mine where I sat with kids and there was literally nothing they could do. There were no walls they could tear apart, a lot of times we just sat and let them know that they weren't going to leave until we took care of it. We ignored a lot of negative behaviors. The teachers used a lot of immediate reinforcement, long-term reinforcement, as well as token economy, and a point system. And that whole thing really grew and grew and grew to include group activities, teams and things like that; this is where it was by the end of the program.

Although all of the students in the Education Center were academically behind, the program did not focus on remediation of academic deficits. Peter did not see remediation as his program's goal, nor academic deficits as the primary disability of his students, even though the primary criterion for returning an Education Center student to a regular classroom situation was the child's academic performance, which needed to be, according to Stein, "not necessarily on grade level, but at least the kid was assuming some responsibility and had some interest and was motivated to learn . . . . If a kid was behaviorally ready, academically behind, and there was a school that had a specialist that was willing to work with him and a resource teacher, we put him back."

The lack of focus on developing children's intellectual skills seen in the original Education Center set a pattern of programming that would be continued when this program moved to the Evers school. Poor school performance was seen as another symptom of the child's illness. Both were believed to be the result of being raised by a single mother in a culture of poverty. In spite of this belief, neither Stein nor Dr. Flagg proposed that this program include offering supports to these children's families in either a psychological or a material sense.

Evers' Education Center

The movement of the Education Center from its downtown location to Evers did not happen because of a philosophical move toward programming for children in a least restrictive environment. Rather, the move took place as the result of other political, economic, and social events that were unfolding at the time. Peter Stein lost his job in the Fall of 1976 because, he believes, of his long standing conflict with the supervisor of the C.A.A. In the Spring of 1977 the program was moved to Evers. Stein perceived this move to have occurred for the following reasons:

> By around the late '70s, community action agencies were beginning to lose money. It wasn't the "Great Society" anymore. So, money was being cut back. That was an expensive building and it was costing the agency a lot of money. The school district was paying the teachers' salaries and for some of the supplies. As long as the program was bringing in big bucks, it was worth it. You see, the teachers' salaries, any kind of investment that comes from another agency is an in-kind donation. Every time you get a federal buck, you get to match it with a local one. So we had more than paid our way and they thought they could kick in the building. But, after awhile, they couldn't justify the outrageous amount of money it was costing.

By 1977, federal and state mandates had established an official designation for students who exhibited the characteristics of many of those who, until then, had attended the Education Center. Funds would be provided by states to districts that served these children in special education programs that followed regulations regarding identification, placement, teacher certification, class size, and the development of an Individualized Educational Program (I.E.P.) for each student. Moving the program away from its downtown location and into Evers put the Education Center fully under the jurisdiction of the school district. The Lakeside schools' special education department was now in charge, and the label attached to the students in the program was changed from "Lakeside Academic Rehabilitation" to "severely emotionally disturbed." Although the new designation was no more accurate in its description of the children than had been the former label, the Severely Emotionally Disturbed label enabled the school district to qualify for funds under new state regulations based on and supported by P.L. 94–142. Poverty program monies were disappearing rapidly. By identifying these children as handicapped, the city school district found a new way to provide for difficult to manage children without having to make any dramatic changes in its policies.

In 1977 the Alternative Attendance Program, i.e., voluntary busing to increase racial integration, began in Lakeside. It was also the year in which the "Evers-Jefferson Twin School" was established. The total population of Evers had fallen dramatically. The official explanation given for placing the Education Center at Evers was that the school now had extra space because of its declining enrollment. However, given the school district's attempts to integrate its schools during a period of national sensitivity toward busing, it was also apparent that it would be poor politics to place a group of aggressive and disruptive Black students into a middle class White school. Since Evers was already perceived as a school that served problem children, it seemed to be the school least likely to be disturbed by this program.

By placing the Education Center at Evers, the school district was making an exception to its own rule, which forbade Black students from other attendance areas or other schools to be transferred into this school. All but three of the students sent to the Education Center were Black, and all were boys.The Education Center located at Evers was providing the school district with an escape valve for dealing with those Black children who did not fit into the more traditional schools they now attended because of the Alternative Attendance Program (busing) or because the closing of some smaller schools resulted in the redistricting of these children into other schools. Mrs. Munroe, chair of the school district Committee on the Handicapped, Sub-Committee for Emotional Disturbance, pointed out that referrals to special education were at their highest from 1977 until 1979, the years during which busing and redistricting began.

Although many of the Education Center students in 1977 were from the Evers neighborhood, by the 1979–80 school year, only three of its 34 students were referred directly from Evers. One of the three boys came directly from a residential treatment facility, and another had been at Evers for one year, after having moved into the neighborhood. He had a history of academic failure, behavior problems and retention in the other two schools that he had attended in the city. The third child is described by Evers' staff as being the one child in the program who was "really very disturbed."

It is not that Evers did not have other children who presented problems to their teachers, but rather that the teachers there felt prepared to handle them, with the support of other school personnel. In fact, Evers had, and continues to have, the smallest number of students referred for special education in the city, in spite of the fact that its children represent a population considered to be at risk for learning and behavior disorders. These children might have been perceived as deviant in a more middle-class,

White school, but at Evers they more closely fit the image held by teachers and administrators of their average student.

The relocation of the Education Center to Evers did not significantly change its programming or structure during its first year and a half. Its four classrooms were housed in the older, back wing of the building. Its students arrived and departed on their own buses, and entered and left the building only through designated doors. The double doors separating the Education Center wing from the rest of the building were kept locked. The administration and supervision of the program belonged to the special education staff, as did the ordering of books and supplies.

Mr. Carp was principal during the 1977–78 school year, after having returned from a year's leave of absence. It was during his absence that the Education Center was placed at Evers. In an earlier battle with the special education office, he had tried to integrate children who were labeled as educable mentally retarded into regular classes, rather than segregate them in self-contained special education classrooms. He had also tried to include nonlabeled children in the special education classrooms for part of their day, if they could benefit from some of the services offered there. The special education office would not permit this kind of programming. Now, in his last year at Evers, he chose not to confront the downtown office over a similar issue.

By the Fall of 1978, changes were beginning at Evers that would have a direct impact on the Education Center. The new principal that year was a Black woman who had been raised in Lakeside. She saw herself as responsible for the total school's operation, which, in her mind, included the Education Center. The doors separating the wings were unlocked, and Education Center children began to eat in the cafeteria with the rest of the school. The population of the school had fallen to approximately 400 students because of the transferring out of the fifth and sixth grades to Jefferson. Evers was now an Early Education Center, and plans for the prekindergarten and full-day kindergarten programs were underway. A Resource Room program for students labeled as emotionally disturbed had also begun, and Evers had become "total *Distar*."

Jean Smith, the instructional specialist, described what she and the resource teacher, Carole Wando, went through in setting up the process by which Education Center students were to be included in regular classrooms:

> We had a meeting with the Special Education Department and the teachers and the regular education teachers and we discussed it. We decided that a fair compromise would be no more than two kids being mainstreamed in a room at one time. So the teachers do expect to have possibly two kids being mainstreamed in their room. That way we were able to deal with the special

education teachers saying, "Hey, you're forcing this kid to be stuck in special education another year. He needs to be mainstreamed." And the regular education teachers saying, "Hey, it's not that easy." So we agreed on a compromise and they are expecting to have kids.

The special education teachers with whom I spoke were not completely satisfied with the compromise, but saw it as a step in the right direction. One of their chief complaints was that students would be mainstreamed only if they could fit into the classes as they existed. Therefore, integration was not being used for the purpose of teaching these children appropriate behavior. Rather, children would be integrated only when they were no longer perceived as deviant by regular classroom teachers. This would not be as difficult at Evers as it would have been at most other schools. Betty Olds, an Education Center teacher, expressed her perception of the mainstreaming program in the following way:

> I feel like it was one way. I never had the feeling of resenting it or any negative thing. That's just the way it is. The onus is on us to modify the kids to fit into that mold. I think that we had the square pegs and we're the ones that had to round it out.

This "rounding out" included the requirement that the special education students' academic skills match those of the students in the regular classroom in which they were placed. Because the academic skills of the "average" Evers student were below grade level, it was easier for the academically below-average Education Center students to be integrated into these classrooms than it would have been those in other elementary schools in Lakeside. The Education Center's adoption of *Distar* as its approach for reading, math and language allowed a special education student to be "plugged into" a "slot" in a regular classroom's *Distar* lesson close to the one he had been receiving in the Education Center. This was also perceived as a means of reassuring the regular classroom teacher that the student had received skills and behavioral training similar to those of the other students in his or her class.

Jean Smith explained that the regular classroom teacher was not given any special preparation for the mainstreamed child's academic needs other than, perhaps, an explanation of some of the peculiarities of a child's specific learning style. She cites the child's severely emotionally disturbed label as the reason for the lack of focus on the child's intellectual functioning:

> Instruction-wise, not too much is done because of the fact that the students are emotionally disturbed rather than academically handicapped. Usually we

try to place students in an instructional group that they can function in. We ask the teacher to expect the student to be able to function academically as the rest of the class does.

Her understanding of the emotional disturbance label also influenced her selection of *Distar* for use by the Education Center classes:

> Special education can get whatever textbooks they want with their textbook money, but we agreed it would be easier [for everyone to use *Distar*] because the kids are emotionally disturbed and not retarded. Whereas, in that case, the kids might need to have special books. We have them in the same books as the regular classes.

The label of severely emotionally disturbed, therefore, exerted another powerful biasing influence that manifested itself in the lack of focus on these students' academic needs in their special education classroom. The Education Center, contrary to its name, turned its attention toward altering its students' "maladaptive behaviors" and "poor social adjustment." After all, as Jean Smith stated, "these kids are emotionally disturbed and not [mentally] retarded." This approach often resulted in students falling even further behind in their academic skill development. Failure and frustration were, however, never cited as explanations for misbehavior by these children.

The psychodynamic and behavioral orientations of the individuals who had established this program certainly played a part in its lack of focus on cognitive skills. However, there is also a tendency in Lakeside to hold low expectations toward the achievement of Black children in general. It is not surprising to Lakeside teachers or school officials when a Black child, particularly a poor, Black child from a single-parent family, performs below average on academic tasks. If such a child's behavior begins to get out of hand, it is explained in terms of his "pathological" upbringing or socialization rather than his frustration with school work. Once the child becomes identified as severely emotionally disturbed, all subsequent "negative" behaviors may become defined in these terms.

Although Evers' teachers, for the most part, have learned to attach a somewhat different meaning to the negative behavior of Black children than is often the case in other elementary schools, this perspective changes even at Evers, once a teacher is faced with a child who has been identified as severely emotionally disturbed. There is still the expectation that the behavior of this child will be qualitatively different from that of the average Evers student. Regular classroom teachers did not feel that behavior problems were inevitable in their classrooms. They developed methods of approaching their children that would not reinforce the negative expectations held elsewhere. They believed they could control their students. They felt this might not be the case, however, for a "severely" disturbed child. However, once Education Center students were mainstreamed, the regular classroom teachers did not see these students as that different from many of their other students.

The Education Center teachers, on the other hand, expected that all their students would be "acting out." After all, that was why these students had been placed there. None of these teachers believed that their classrooms could operate in the smooth, well-organized fashion that was typical of most regular classrooms at Evers. Betty Olds, a special education teacher, expressed this understanding in the following way:

> It's difficult for me to sometimes keep my standards in line. You know, I don't want to set them too high. But I don't want to compromise either. So, it's a constant battle. So, in other words, I would love for them to be like Mary's class [second grade], but if I expected that of them it would be mass mutiny. They can't do it. That's why they're here in the first place.

In expecting some of her students to be "bad," Betty made allowances for the kinds of disruptive behavior that characterized the students assigned to her room.

As we will see, the teachers in the Education Center varied in the degree to which they understand that an "expectation cycle" influenced the operation of their classrooms. Their personal orientations largely directed the focus of their programs toward either behavioral control or the establishment of a positive relationship with their students. Interventions were directed toward working with the child in the classroom. Although each teacher recognized to varying degrees that the problem behaviors she or he saw in the classroom were often the results of interactions elsewhere, communication with both the home and other, regular teachers was not seen as her or his role.

Instead, a social worker was assigned to coordinate the other services needed by the Education Center students. This woman, Laurie, a White woman in her early thirties, had been raised in a wealthy family. Her training was not in social work, but in special education. She frequently expressed a perspective similar to that of Dr. Flagg, and presented a very pessimistic picture of the children at Evers and their families. In fact, she believed that almost all the regular classroom students at Evers could be classified as emotionally disturbed.

Although a major part of Laurie's role in the Education Center was to work with the families of its students, she talked continually about how impossible it was for her to communicate with them:

You know, you really have to be humble when you see some of these people and the things they live with. What do I know about living like that? I drive into the neighborhood in my Mercedes and then go back to my house in the suburbs. Nothing that I can do or say is going to matter. Can't blame them for not listening to me.

She now "works with" only the "good parents," i.e., those that cooperate, and "deals with" the others only when absolutely necessary. This includes having them sign papers such as permission forms and Individual Education Programs. She does not believe that most of these children's mothers are capable of understanding the complexities of the program, and so tells them only what she must and does so in a way that gets parents to do what she feels is most expedient.

Laurie believed that the most effective methods for dealing with the inappropriate behavior she saw in students from the Education Center were those that showed the children that she was as tough as they were. Corporal punishment and strong "street language" were what "these kids are used to. They are aggressive kids from aggressive homes and it's the only thing they can really relate to." She believed that she was placed in her position as coordinator of the program because, as she put it, "I don't take any crap from kids. They know downtown that if any kid starts trouble with me, I won't hesitate to put him down on the floor. That's what these kids need."

As Dan Pallard's and Barbara Sheppard's special education classrooms are discussed in the following pages, it is important to keep in mind that the supportive services that these teachers requested were administered through Laurie. Her administration limited the program to isolated classrooms offering limited support outside of the class. Her predominant mode of support came in the form of "crisis intervention," which meant removing the child from the classroom for isolation in the "time-out" room in her office. Laurie would then decide if the proper intervention would involve ignoring the child, talking to him, paddling, or, when all else failed, taking him home.

Dan Pallard's Classroom

The data that follow, taken from field notes, describe the interactions between two boys, Tyrone and Bobby, which took place during a two-hour period spent in Dan Pallard's special education classroom. As the events occur, Mr. Pallard, a White man in his mid-thirties, wearing corduroy jeans and a plaid shirt, is sitting at his desk, partially hidden behind a file cabinet and a bookcase. He is working with another student. This private space was created so that the teacher could meet with students individually, either to discuss their concerns, resolve problems, or work on academic skills. The rest of the classroom is divided by the arrangement of furniture. Ten student desks and chairs are set in short rows, facing a chalkboard that has the day's schedule written on it. Behind these desks are two small round tables, where small groups of two or three children sometimes work together with the teacher aide, following the curriculum set out in the texts and workbooks they were assigned. To the left of this area is the *Distar* corner, with a semicircle of chairs facing the teacher's chair. *Distar* books and dittoed worksheets are placed on an adjacent table.

When Mr. Pallard's classroom was moved from the old, back wing into the main building in 1980, his second year at Evers, he did not change the physical arrangement of the classroom. Although the new room was brighter because of its new paint and fluorescent lights, it still lacked decoration. In both rooms, there was little in the way of creative arts projects, science materials, or extra reading materials. Student papers were sometimes pinned onto a bulletin board. Pictures of outdoor scenes cut from a travel calendar and a black cardboard chart with white capital and lower case letters of the alphabet covered the wall above the chalkboard. In the old room, the windows were translucent. In the new room, there are no windows.

Satticia, the teacher aide, is working with four children, while Mr. Pallard works with Robert, in semiprivacy. Enrolled in this class are eight boys, eight to ten years old, who are all present this day. Individual time is being given to Robert so that he can move at a more rapid pace in his program. He needs to catch up to a reading group in the regular fourth grade class so that he can be recommended to be mainstreamed. The events that follow are not unique to this day or to the two boys focused on in this description. They have been selected as an illustration of behaviors that were typically observed in this class and others in the Education Center:

> One boy (Bobby) comes in the room and asks if he can get his breakfast downstairs. The teacher says yes and the boy gets up and leaves. Another boy comes up and says he wants to go too. He says he has missed his bus and didn't get a chance to eat. Dan (the teacher) lets the other boy go. Two of the others remaining in the room then tell Dan that the second boy (Tyrone) had lied. He had walked to school, didn't miss his bus or his breakfast like he said. He already had breakfast.

> [*Observer's Comment*: Dan is careful not to take the other children's tattling as truth. He knows that they too are capable of lying. The boy who went to get his breakfast second, Tyrone, is a short and cute little boy. He was extremely convincing. I never doubted him and later learned that he *had* lied. This behavior, lying in a very convincing manner, is one that I continue to observe

in this child. Another characteristic that he demonstrates today is always wanting to be with the boy who left first, Bobby. They seem to be like Tweedle Dee and Tweedle Dum. They do all kinds of acting out and lying to be with each other.]

Tyrone and Bobby are sitting together in the center of the room, supposedly working on their workbooks, but neither has started working. Bobby looks up at the door and a boy passing in the hall has stopped and is looking in the room. He looks at the boy and says loudly, "Git out of here, boy!" He turns to Tyrone and they start talking about the work they have to do. Ten minutes have passed since they were to have started working. They have done no work thus far. They are still eating their breakfast at their desks. They continue talking and the teacher calls out, "Tyrone, I think you are supposed to be doing your board work, not working with Bobby. Look at your schedule." This has the effect of quieting the whole room down, but doesn't get these two down to work. One of them just keeps eating. The other takes out some books and papers and on occasion looks up and copies his schedule from the chalk-board . . . .

They have been consistently not working. Bobby gets up and sharpens his pencil. The other boy throws away the breakfast plates. They take out some crayons and talk to each other. Tyrone opens his workbook, "*My City*. Bobby takes out his. Fifteen minutes have passed and they have not started to work. They talk to each other. Tyrone asks Bobby to watch him work. Bobby stands and watches. . . .

Both boys work for a short time, then talk to each other, stop working and laugh. Tyrone then calls out to the aide, "Miss C., I need help." He gets up and walks over to her. She is helping another child with math. Now Bobby, sitting alone, calls out to her three times for help. She turns to Tyrone and then back to the other child. Tyrone then comes to the math table where she has been working with three boys in a math group. They complain, "This is our table." The aide responds, "He can be here too. I'm here to help all of you." The other boys then get into an argument over Tyrone's workbook, one telling the other that he has already finished *My City* and that the book he has now is much harder. He says to Tyrone, "I need help. My work is harder than yours."

[*Observer's Comment:* Satticia Carpenter, the aide, tries to assist the children with their work, but often has difficulty in understanding the assignment. On several occasions she gives them the correct answers. They finally settle down to work for about ten minutes.]

Satticia then announces that it is time for *Distar*. Al has returned to the group, and another child goes to work with Mr. Pallard. The other children, including Bobby and Tyrone, proceed to the *Distar* corner . . . .

The reading group is proceeding smoothly. Suddenly an argument breaks out in the group. The aide becomes angry with them and turns to the teacher and calls out, "Mr. P., Bobby needs to leave the group." Mr. P. gets up and says, "Bobby, you decide if you can stay. You make the decision." Bobby protests, pouts, and pushes his chair back and blames Tyrone as the cause of his problem. Mr. P. says to Bobby, "Did you like it when he disrupted you?" Bobby responds, "Yes." "Well," says Mr. P., "they don't like it when you disrupt them." Bobby responds, "It's not my problem." Mr. P. says, "You make up your mind. If I come over here again, I'll have to take you out of the group." Mr. P. turns away and it is now Tyrone's turn to read.

I notice Bobby put his foot on the edge of the table and give it a slight push toward Tyrone. Tyrone yells out, "He's pushing the table." Mr. P. asks both Tyrone and Bobby to leave the group. Bobby smiles [*Observer's Comment:* These two boys have been together all morning and it is almost as though Bobby would not leave the group unless Tyrone came with him. So the two of them are off now, out of the group, and by themselves.]

Bobby goes to his seat. Tyrone goes to his desk, opens it up, and throws all his stuff on the floor, then picks it up and throws it in the basket.

These notes demonstrate interactions and individual behaviors that were consistently observed in all the special education classes I visited at Evers. Most notable was the contaminating effect of one child's behavior on the others. Satticia described this behavior in the following way:

I don't understand why they are the way they are. They just don't know how to get along with each other nohow. They can't play or share without a fight. You talks to one and then the other gets mad. Tyrone's one of the worst like that and he gets the others to be just like him 'cause of his selfishness.

Dan Pallard never excused disruptions as being atypical, but rather saw them as a fact of life, to be expected from the kinds of children who were placed in his class. They continually demanded attention, support and comfort from the adults in the room. From his perspective, self-contained classes, such as this one, do not give students the opportunity to experience more appropriate behaviors.

I think that if you want the kids to be something else, you have to expose them to that something else or they're not going to know what it is. . . . most of my kids know when they're going to blow up, and if I go over to them and tell them to sit down and cool off, most of them will just do that. And then they'll come back. . . .

But I think that without being exposed to kids acting normally in a classroom, it won't work. Okay, some days in here we have such beautiful days, everybody's just fabulous. And then other days you have one kid who's really in a crummy mood, walks in and you talk to him and it doesn't work out and he sets off like three or four other kids and before you know it you got everybody up for grabs. I think that they have to see the situation in a classroom that doesn't have S.E.D. kids, where if one kid blows, hey, everybody else just ignores it. I don't think they get to see it enough.

Since neither Dan nor his students had the opportunity to interact with typical Evers students when his class was placed in the old wing, he found it difficult to determine which students' behaviors would fit the expectations of the regular classroom teachers. The decision to mainstream a child was based upon the student's academic performance, his immunity to the negative behaviors of others, and his behavior during non-structured, relatively unsupervised activities. In the following statement, Dan describes how he arrived at the decision to try one of his students, Steve, in the mainstreaming program.

> One of the major things we have in here is that minor squabbles between kids can develop into major catastrophes. Everybody is quick to respond verbally to someone else's troubles, and Steve got to a point where he was able to ignore those behaviors if he was working on something. He could keep on task, and if he got off, all I'd have to do was say, "Steve, will you keep busy?" And he'd go right back to work. He didn't continue on. Some of the kids can't stop; once they get into the rut it keeps building up, building up, building up until I have to remove them to someplace. Steve got to the point where he wouldn't indulge himself in those kind of things. Another thing was that he got a lot more confident in his work. He would accept it. He used to complain a lot, "This is too hard, this is. . . ." Before he even saw what he had to do, he would complain about it. And that dwindled almost completely. And then in activities like going on field trips and programs in gym and stuff he was able to handle himself.

During the year that his classroom was placed in the main building, Dan Pallard came to see that many of the children at Evers exhibited behaviors similar to those he saw in his own students:

> You come from that special area and I see less of a difference in my kids this year than the kids in the rest of the building, maybe because I see more of the rest of the building now than I did before. I didn't see behaviors in the rest of the building because I wasn't there and this year I see like, I'll hear a disturbance during lunch hour or something or in the bathroom and I'll say, "Oh my God, what are they up to now?" And I'll go in and it's not my kids. It's somebody else.

A certified special education teacher with six years of previous teaching experiences in another city, Dan did not believe that any of his children were "mentally ill." He saw them, rather, as children, responding in normal ways to the circumstances of their lives. Some of these circumstances were dramatic, as in the case of Tyrone, who at five years old had spent three years living on the streets of another small Northeastern city with his eight year old brother. Others were more typical examples of children living under conditions of extreme poverty, despair and confusion. Dan explains:

> You know, it blows my mind how well some of these kids are doing. I don't know if I could do that well if I had to live in some of those situations. Some

of the homes are real nice, but some are so disorganized. Craziness! I just couldn't handle the situation. You walk into Tom's house, he's the White kid in here, and the front room is just boxes. They are piled from the floor to the ceiling. Then you walk into another room and there's a couch with all this stuff all over the place. And the kitchen! There are seven cats and dogs running all over the house. Everybody is screaming at each other constantly. I've been there three times. It's been like that every time, and I leave feeling crazy.

In each case, this teacher believed that it would be through the relationship that he established with individual children that the strength to cope with their lives would develop. Finally, though, they needed to behave in ways that would allow them to participate in normal childhood activities if they were ever to break out of the cycle of failure in which they were now stuck. As Dan put it:

I explained to the kids, I say, "It's all a game. This whole thing is a game. All our lives, everything. You have to learn how to act in each different situation."

Deficient academic performance would also limit the opportunity for Dan's students to be part of a regular classroom. During the ten months that I observed his classrooms, only one student left for a less restrictive setting. Another was sent to a residential treatment facility. Combining a lack of focus on academic skills, contagious acting-out behavior, no appropriate peer models, low expectations and inconsistent behavior management with stressful home environments was certainly the right formula to assure that few, if any, of the students in Dan Pallard's class would ever be successfully integrated into a regular school program.

Barbara Sheppard's Classroom

A former school administrator and remedial reading teacher, Barbara Sheppard is a White woman in her late thirties. In the Spring of 1980, she replaced a teacher who had resigned from the Education Center. Mrs. Sheppard had never taught a special education class nor had any training in teaching children with behavior problems. The highly structured behavioral approach she followed during the Fall and Winter months that I spent as a participant-observer in her new classroom in the main wing of the Evers school, developed as the result of the often-devastating experiences of the previous school year.

Although I was unable to directly observe her classroom during its first year here (I was told she was having a difficult time controlling her class, and it was "recommended" that I not observe her room), what I did often see in passing her room was a group of noisy children arguing with each other and paying little if any attention to whatever lessons were being presented. Mrs. Sheppard, both in her first and second year, was seen in angry confrontations with several different students, yelling at them and often using corporal punishments, including twisting children's arms and forcing them to the floor, pulling their hair, and/or paddling.

The following incident took place during Barbara's first year in the Education Center:

> The door to Laurie's room is thrown open (I was taping an interview with the social worker at the time). Barbara Sheppard, a tall, well-dressed and meticulously groomed White woman, is holding a chubby, eight year old, very dark-skinned Black boy, Michael Thomas, firmly by the arm, and she pushes him into the room. "Where's the paddle?" she says, red-faced and not noticing, at first, that I am in the room. "He has been mouthing off at me all day and I've had it. At the concert this morning Michael embarrassed the whole class by his behavior. Using foul language and cutting up. I should have put him right out then and there, but I didn't want to add to the class' embarrassment in front of all those people."

> Laurie gets up out of her seat and walks around her desk to Barbara and Michael. "I think you ought to know that this is all being taped" [*Observer's Comment:* Barbara seems oblivious to this remark. Her anger and outrage are obvious. Her face fluctuates from red to white and her hands are trembling. Laurie's remarks seem to indicate that what is about to occur here should not be recorded for posterity.]

> Laurie takes a traditional wooden paddle from its hook on the wall. "Bend over," yells Barbara at the child. Laurie interrupts, "Wait a minute. I really don't think that you ought to be taping this. You had better turn it off right now. I don't want any problems from the district about anything that goes on here (I turn off the tape recorder.) Okay, now let's hear about this." Barbara appears to have calmed down somewhat. . . . However, she grabs the boy by his arm, turns him around, lifts up his sweater, which hung down over his pants, and gives him three very hard swats on the rear end. "This time it was three, but next time it will be 40—I mean five or six. I kept telling him to stop all day. Finally, during language, I had enough. So I went over to him and gave him a swat. And do you know what he did? He hit me back. No child ever lays a hand on me."
> [*Observer's Comments:* Michael did not say a word, nor demonstrate any overt emotional response.]

> Barbara puts down the paddle and Laurie turns to her and says, "Well, I think we should call his mother and let her know what he's been doing." There is still the same stone-faced expression on Michael's face, and he has not spoken a word. Laurie goes to the telephone and dials. "Hello, is your mother there? May I speak with her, please?" She turns to Michael, grabs him by the arm, and pulls him toward the telephone. She has a large plaster cast on her right arm, which runs from the wrist to above the elbow. She lifts this arm over his head and comes down hard and swiftly on the top of his head. The impact

causes a loud clonking noise, and Michael finally reacts. He moves his hand to the spot where Laurie's cast landed and rubs his head. Tears begin to well in his eyes.

Laurie speaks: "Come here and tell your mother what you have been doing. Tell her the names you have been calling Mrs. Sheppard. Why don't you call your mother those names? You wouldn't do that, now, would you?" Michael's mother has come to the phone, and Laurie tells her, "I had to call you because Michael is giving us a lot of trouble. First of all, he was thrown off the school bus and then he was impossible with his teacher. We cannot put up with this behavior. I thought you should know about all this and talk to him." She hands Michael the phone, and for the first time, he speaks: "Hello, mamma." Large tears now spill out of his eyes and down his cheeks. Laurie turns to Barbara, smiling, and whispers loud enough for both Michael and me to hear, "Look, he's crying." She then moves to Michael's side and speaks into the ear that is not being held to the telephone. Apparently, his mother is speaking to him in his other ear. With what can best be described as a provoking tone, Laurie says, "Go ahead. Call your mother the names you called the teacher. Go ahead. No, you wouldn't use that language with her. So why should your teacher have to put up with it? Go ahead, tell her and see how she likes it." (Michael does not react, except for the tears streaking his face.)

The impact of the punishment imposed on Michael and the paddlings often administered to other boys in the Education Center cannot be completely understood without considering their racial implications. Michael's holding back any visible expression of emotion until the blow to his head overwhelmed him is similar to behavior described elsewhere (Grier & Cobbs, 1968; Silverstein & Krate, 1975) as a survival strategy into which Black children have been socialized in the United States. In Michael's case, the disciplinary tactics reportedly used by Michael's mother had been reinforced by both Laurie and Barbara. Control over his immediate overt behavior had been achieved at the risk of feeding the rage that may be growing within this child.

As a consequence of this and similar, though less dramatic incidents, Barbara realized that if she was to keep teaching in this program, she needed to develop strategies that would help her control students' behavior. And so, during the summer of 1980, she enrolled in a course in behavior modification. There she learned that in order to operate a well-behaved classroom, clear, straightforward rules needed to be established. The children needed to understand the consequence of following or breaking rules. Since it was assumed that the rules themselves would have little intrinsic value to her students, external reinforcers needed to be provided. Following the rules meant getting a reward. Disobedience meant no reward, or relinquishing some of the rewards that had already been accumulated.

In order for a reward to be truly reinforcing, it needed to be highly valued. What could be more powerful reinforcers for these children than money and food? And so, Barbara developed a complex system in which points, checks, and stars accumulated throughout the day could be traded, twice a day, for money. This money would be kept in each child's personal class bank, held by the teacher, and could be used, twice a day, in the classroom store. The children could choose to buy school supplies, toys, and comic books or save their money for a special trip for pizza or hamburgers with the teacher or her aide. However, the most preferred reward was food (raisins, fruit, juice, cookies, etc.). The children particularly preferred those foods that involved some preparation by Barbara or her aide, Sue, a young White woman. Toast and peanut butter, grilled cheese sandwiches, milk shakes, and hot chocolate would be prepared in the classroom for the boy who had enough money in his bank. Since no other snack was given in the classroom during the day, and none of the boys brought in food from home (all received free breakfast and lunch), food was, to say the least, an appealing reinforcer.

Although Barbara recognized that the kinds of rewards she had selected for her students were the kind they would strive for, she attributed the "success" of her new classroom to its high degree of structure. She explains:

> Well, everything is pretty structured as far as they know. There are rewards for this, there are consequences for that, you know, and if you don't have a good day it's nobody's fault but your own. If you want to have a perfect day, these are the rules; follow the rules, you can get a star every day, Last year we just gave points in our room at 10:30, 12:30 and 2:00. It was three times a day. And that was really tough to remember. 'cause I might say at 9:00 "You've lost a point. See." And I'd have to remember until 10:30 or maybe he grew up and really got it together and here you're this good kid at 10:30 and now I have to remember an hour ago how bad you were. I have to take the points away. Now they're angry all over again. Now I do it for every single lesson. And they tell you as you go through the day. If you get within five of a perfect score, 27 out of 32 or better, 32 is perfect and then I always allow five. So anywhere between 27 and 32, that person gets a star for the day. There are separate points for "work" and for "behavior." They get just behavior points for lunch and for the beginning of the day. Those are times I don't control.

The physical organization of Barbara's classroom reflects the structured approach she has adopted. Ten student desks were arranged in five rows of two, each desk facing the front chalkboard (There were ten students in her class, nine and ten years old). On this blackboard, students' names were listed, followed by a work schedule for the day, which each student must copy onto a dittoed "schedule sheet" placed on his desk before he arrives each morning. On the wall over the chalkboard, to the left of the students' desks, and extending the entire width of the room, was a chart entitled "Our Class Rules." These rules were broken down into two categories,

"Work" and "Behavior." The students' adherence to these regulations determined the number of points given on their individual work schedules.

Barbara's desk was located to the right of the students' desks, and the teacher aide's desk behind them. A large round table sat at the back of the room; it was used for small-group instruction. The familiar semicircle of student chairs facing an adult-sized chair was placed in the rear right-hand corner of the room, next to the small bookcase containing *Distar* materials. There were few frills in the room, i.e., no art work or other projects. In spite of this, the room had a homey quality, probably because of the many houseplants hanging from its fluorescent light fixtures (there are no windows in this room). The toaster and blender in the back of the room, used to prepare food reinforcers, added to this feeling.

Although Mrs. Sheppard developed a greater degree of control in her new classroom, instances of students' outbursts, e.g., throwing over desks, tearing up papers, cursing at each other and/or teachers, continued. These were dealt with by denying the acting-out child his points. On occasion, the loss of points was followed by another angry outburst, which Barbara handled by reminding the child that he would continue to lose more points if he did not get himself under control. This worked to control their behavior during my observation, but Barbara reports that on occasion she still resorts to paddling or sending a child home because he "loses it." The point system seems to work well in minimizing the contagious effect that one child's behavior was seen to have on that of the others. Barbara would remind the other children that if they joined the misbehaving child in breaking the rules, then they too would lose points.

Her approach can be described as focusing on control, i.e., creating a controlled environment, which in turn controls the children's behavior. Although there were occasionally times in the day when the children discussed with each other and their teacher the problems they may have had, this was less significant than was the behavioral system that was consistent and constant component of the life of this classroom. Unlike Dan Pallard, Barbara Sheppard never mentioned discussions with the children as an important ingredient of her classroom, nor did she discuss meeting with the children's families. She had met with all the children's mothers at least once, as mandated by state law when developing each child's Individual Educational Program. However, any additional contacts with them were made only if the student was in a crisis. Barbara believed that the difficulties her students have in school are related to their lives outside of school. She did not see their academic deficits as being responsible for their negative behavior, in spite of the fact that all her students were functioning below what would be expected from children of their chronological age. However, she did not believe that her students were "mentally ill," and questioned the appropriateness of their being labeled severely emotionally disturbed.

Barbara: When I first took over the classroom last March, when they told me they were severely emotionally handicapped, I thought they'd be like schizophrenic and psychotic and all these kinds of things. And to me they're just more behaviorally disturbed.

Question: How do you make that distinction?

Barbara: I guess that the majority of them I deal with deal with reality and have awareness of the system, okay, of life. But just have not learned how to control their behavior. And perhaps some of the problem is that they're coming from environments that don't have structure. And I used to point that out a lot, especially last spring, with the ones that were so hostile and rebelled so much to the rules and regulations in the large big world and that you need to follow them. Learn to follow them now, and learn to pay the consequences when you don't. Because that's what's going to happen when you grow up. So most of them, I feel, it's just a matter of trying to deal with anger and when things don't go your way, coping with them. For the most part, I think then they could go back to a regular classroom.

In spite of the fact that neither the special education teachers or classroom aides from the Education Center, the majority of regular classroom teachers at Evers, its principal, social worker, school psychologist, nor the chairperson of the district Committee on the Handicapped believe that these students are "really" emotionally disturbed, removing this label became a nearly impossible task. The next chapter will trace the career of two Education Center students, Michael Thomas, the child who was punished in Laurie's office, and Carl Smith, a child who had been successfully mainstreamed out of the Education Center into Mary Flynn's second-grade classroom at Evers, and back to his referring school. This will help clarify how some children in Lakeside came to be identified as disturbed and illustrate some of the consequences of their being labeled.

6

Labeling in Lakeside

Who Gets Labeled?

The procedure by which students are referred to and placed in special education programs is generally thought of as an event that assures that students with special needs will receive an education that is appropriate. The outcome of this procedure is believed to be the proper response to the students' handicapping conditions. However, in the case of those in Lakeside who became identified as severely emotionally disturbed, more than the students' condition was responsible for their eventual placement in special education classes. The school district's definition of deviant behavior contributed significantly to this process. This definition does not violate any federal or state laws; on the contrary, the school district's procedures manual follows legal mandates to the letter. However, as has been demonstrated, events of the past 20 have had a significant influence on this school district's definition of emotional disturbance.

Table 6.1 illustrates that during the 1980–81 school year, 25 percent of all students designated as handicapped in Lakeside (total school population of approximately 22,000) had been identified as emotionally disturbed. This is a significantly higher percentage than was the case on a national level during the same year. The U.S. General Accounting Office found that nationally in the 1980–81 school year only eight percent of all students identified as handicapped under P.L. 94–142 were classified as emotionally disturbed.

The data in Table 6.1 were gathered by the chairperson of the Subcommittee on Emotional Disturbance of the school district's Committee on the Handicapped. They were sent to the state's Special Education Department, and included students placed in self-contained classrooms as well as those served by resource teachers and other support personnel while enrolled in regular classrooms. Approximately 60 percent of this district's "handicapped" population are not, however, in self-contained classes, but are placed in regular classrooms and receive supportive services from special education resource teachers. These include children who have been labeled as

93

TABLE 6.1

Numbers and Approximate Percentage of All Lakeside Special Education
Students by Handicapping Condition, December, 1980

Handicapping Condition	# of Students	% of Total
Educable Mentally Retarded	602	30%
Emotionally Disturbed	507	25%
Learning Disabled	275	14%
All Others	646	31%
TOTAL	2,030	100%

educable mentally retarded (E.M.R.), learning disabled (L.D.) or emotionally disturbed (E.D.).

The official statistics compiled by the district's research department to
"provide a history of Black student enrollment," underestimated the actual
numbers of Black students receiving special education services. This set of
statistics deals only with the 975 students enrolled in self-contained special
education classes during the 1980–81 school year. Among these students,
44 percent were Black, as compared to the total Black enrollment in the
district of 33 percent. These 975 students do not include the majority of
students in Lakeside who have been identified as handicapped and labeled
as either E.M.R., L.D., or E.D. and placed in regular classrooms. The
disproportionate number of Black students who have been identified as
handicapped are therefore underrepresented by this set of statistics.

Mrs. Munroe, the chairperson of the Lakeside school district's Subcommittee on Emotional Disturbance, had presided over all meetings of the
district's Committee on the Handicapped during 1980 at which children
were labeled emotionally disturbed. She stated that the large majority of
children labeled as emotionally disturbed were Black. In addition, she
estimated that 67 percent of E.M.R. students were Black, of which two
thirds were boys. 75 percent of these students came from low-income families. In comparison, among students labeled as learning disabled, approximately 75 percent were White, most were boys, and only 40 percent were
poor. These estimates correspond to data gathered on a national level that
also indicate that Blacks are overrepresented among children labeled as
E.M.R. and suggest that these children might be underrepresented among
the learning disabled (U.S. General Accounting Office, 1981).

Black students were even more overrepresented among children labeled
as emotionally disturbed in this district than they were among those labeled E.M.R. Of those identified as severely emotionally disturbed, 80
percent were Black, 87 percent male, and 99 percent poor. This group of
students had also elevated the total number of Black students enrolled in
self-contained special education classes. However, among students with

other handicapping conditions who were placed in segregated special education programs, the numbers of Black students were not significantly different from their numbers in the general population. These include classes for severely impaired, physically handicapped children, trainable mentally retarded children, the deaf, the blind, and the multiply handicapped.

Labeling a child as *severely* emotionally disturbed carries an even more intense connotation regarding "illness" than does the unqualified emotional disturbance label. This designation is often, in other school districts, reserved for those children whose behavior and social functioning would be considered deviant and dysfunctional in most cultures. These "psychotic" or "autistic-like" children until recently have not, in Lakeside, been included among those labeled as severely emotionally disturbed. When, in 1981, a class for psychotic and autistic-like children was developed and placed at the Evers school, it became designated as the Withdrawn–Severely Emotionally Disturbed class, so as to distinguish its students from those who had traditionally been labeled as severely emotionally disturbed in Lakeside.

The typical child identified as severely emotionally disturbed in Lakeside is a Black boy who comes from a low-income, single-parent, female-headed household. The majority of their families are subsidized under Aid to Families with Dependent Children. A substantial number of the children labeled as disturbed live in foster homes or have been placed in foster care at one time or another in their lives. Their behavior has been disruptive to the normal operation of the classroom from which they had been referred. Most are perceived as aggressive, angry, and defiant. Mrs. Munroe believes that the severe emotional disturbance label has been used as a means of providing programs for children who are difficult to manage, while relieving classroom teachers from having to deal with children from, as she put it, "a different culture."

Mrs. Munroe and most of the other people interviewed (the exceptions being the school district psychiatrist, Dr. Flagg, and several psychologists) believed that only a very few of the children labeled either as emotionally disturbed or severely emotionally disturbed were "really disturbed." She believed that the majority of children labeled S.E.D. displayed behaviors which scared teachers. They question adult authority, express their feelings openly, and are more aggressive with each other than most teachers are able to tolerate. Her familiarity with children labeled severely emotionally disturbed extended beyond her role as a chairperson of the district's Committee on the Handicapped. She had also been a teacher in the Education Center when it was first established to serve difficult-to-manage children through the Lakeside Community Action Agency. When this program was moved to the Evers school and became a special education program for children identified as severely emotionally disturbed, Mrs. Munroe followed as a teacher on special assignment. Based on these experiences, she believes that the kinds of behaviors that result in special education placements are not symptoms of disturbance, but rather are more typical of low-income, Black, male children than of the White middle class child.

Her years at Evers, and her subsequent role as supervisor of the district Committee on the Handicapped, led Mrs. Munroe to realize that both a school's principal and its overall culture strongly influence a school's tolerance for deviance. This tolerance is not seen as an acceptance of the aggressive, antisocial behavior often defined as "disturbed," but rather as a school's willingness to deal with problem behaviors instead of referring them elsewhere. Evers was identified as the school with the lowest number of referrals of students for special education in spite of the fact that its students represent the population most often found in special education placements in Lakeside. This phenomenon operates in many inner-city schools with populations similar to that of Evers:

> Logically, this type of school should tolerate a broader diversity even of misbehaviors and lower intellectual potency. "Deviancy" is defined phenomenologically by teachers and administrators, although it is also a reflection of the school structure. Empirically, it probably can be related to frequency of referral for possible placement of children in classes for the emotionally disordered, the mildly retarded, etc. (Budoff, 1972, p. 201)

Mrs. Munroe, the principal of Evers, and many of the teachers, parents, and other school personnel with whom I spoke, related a school's ability to handle diversity in children to its understanding of the children's "culture." By understanding deviant behavior within the context of the totality of the child's experiences, it is no longer perceived as evidence of a disturbance, but rather as the result of the child's "not knowing the rules." In the following statement, Mrs. Rivers, the principal of Evers, expressed her understanding of this phenomenon as it has occurred in Lakeside and, in particular, as it relates to Evers' ability to work with "difficult" children:

> We can "mainstream" here because our teachers are aware of the kids' cultural differences. The school that can't handle them can't do so because they can't accept cultural difference. Most of the elementary schools are really much better now than they used to be, because of the busing and the closing of schools which caused redistributing students. Often schools assume that Black kids are Alternative Attendance students, but they are really part of their neighborhood now, because of the redistricting of neighborhoods. We just had a case of a school wanting us to take a kid here who was having problems and is in the fourth grade for the second time. They feel

it's too bad we're not up to the sixth grade so that he could come here. They don't want to label him—just send him here because "You have more services there." That's a lot of crap. We have no more services than any other school. The truth is that his sister is here and is doing well here, but was failing in their school. So they think he'll do better here. The funny part is that he's really one of their kids, and they think he's an Alternative Attendance student.

Although administrators set the tone for their school and have been seen to be vital in decision making with regard to the referral and placement of children in special education, the tolerance and expectations of teachers are essential factors that determine whether or not a child is perceived as deviant (Algozzine, 1977; Algozzine & Curran, 1979; Curran, 1977; Ross & Salvia, 1975). A building principal can certainly move his or her staff in a direction that provides for an understanding of their students' needs, as well as appropriate programs within that school. However, it is individual classroom teachers who are charged with carrying out these programs.

Evers' teachers expect that their students will behave "inappropriately." However, they also expect that they will be able to handle their students' misbehavior. During the past 20 years, programs and approaches have developed at this school that assist the teacher in the management of his or her students. Teachers at Evers do not view the Black child's open display of emotion or rejection of authority as a symptom of an illness. These behaviors are understood as examples of a lack of "appropriate" social skills. This definition of their students' behavior has allowed teachers to confront misbehaving students directly and provide direct instruction in social skills. Operating with this understanding has eliminated the insecurity and fear experienced by teachers at other schools in Lakeside when confronted by an angry, Black male child.

Mrs. Rivers, Evers' principal and a Black woman who was raised in Lakeside, sees the escalating misbehavior of Black male children as the outcome of White females' fear of dealing with these boys' misbehavior:

> The White female teachers are afraid to deal with Black males, even when they are little boys. The Black girls are either dealt with directly or ignored because they don't present too much of a threat. But, dealing with the Black male is another issue. My husband made me aware of how much an issue this is, and I saw it happen with my own children. Teachers would deal with my daughter, but were afraid to deal with my son in ways that he needed to be dealt with. The same thing happened in the school where I used to be principal. When a Black male child had behavior problems, they were immediately referred. That's why we have all boys in the S.E.D. program.

One of the school psychologists at Evers believes that when the child sees that his misbehavior causes the teacher to respond with fear, he may believe he has the upper hand in their interaction. The child then may play the role of the "crazy nigger." The psychologist explains:

> There's a phenomenon in the Black community called being a "crazy nigger." This term is used to refer to someone who's acting in a certain kind of way to intimidate others. It's used as a special tactic. It convinces others to behave in the way that the person acting "crazy" wants him to. So, if a person or a kid starts acting berserk people will stay away from him and will not expect this person to act in any other kind of way. People make the statement, "What can you expect from that crazy nigger?" I feel that this is operating for some of the kids here who have been labeled as severely emotionally disturbed.

A resource teacher at another elementary school in Lakeside explained this phenomenon in terms of some classroom teachers' lack of management skills:

> Aggression is in the eye of the beholder. The Black kid is probably no more aggressive than the White kid. It's really a matter of who owns the problem. The kids I get in here for "cooling-out" all come from the same three classrooms. They're the rooms with the discipline problems. There is physical chaos in these rooms and it's not clear to the kids what's expected of them. Their kids are no more tough than any others. They just can't deal with them.

Mr. Brown, the teacher of the bilingual/bicultural classroom at the same school, feels that the problems encountered by Black male children in the Lakeside schools often relate to the teachers' misinterpretation of the child's behavior, which sets up a negative chain reaction:

> Question: Why do you think that Black boys are identified as Emotionally Disturbed more often than Whites?
>
> Mr. Brown: You have to understand the interchange that occurs. A kid has a problem and the teacher calls him out. Then the kid gives the teacher a *look*. The teacher interprets it as a lack of respect. If you're hung up on it, and many teachers are, that's where the trouble begins. You have to understand kids and what they're telling you and not be hung up with your own interpretation of what they mean. Gary [a former Education Center student, now in Mr. B's class] has a problem with other teachers. They insist on an answer and he has trouble with that. They take it as disrespect, but he's a very withdrawn, nonverbal type of a kid, and if he's pushed, he becomes frustrated. I never understood why he was special ed. until I saw how some teachers were dealing with him and the behavior that resulted. That's a problem with lots of teachers in this school. They don't understand the kids and how they react.

These perspectives reflect what these individuals and others have experienced in their years of working in Lakeside public schools. These statements focus on the teacher's role in the interaction that has occurred between the teacher and the student. It would be inaccurate to conclude that the teacher is therefore *completely* responsible for the child's problematic behavior. Obviously the child is a partner in the interaction. The other environments in which he functions (e.g., home, community) may also serve as reinforcers of those behaviors that are perceived as deviant within the school. However, because the teacher is in a position of power in interaction with the student, it is the teacher's definition of the student's behavior that results in the eventual labeling of the child as "disturbed."

Labeling the Education Center Students

Each boy came to the Education Center by a similar route. Each started his school career in a regular classroom, in a school other than Evers. Examination of the records of the students in the two classes for students labeled severely emotionally disturbed at Evers, known collectively as the Education Center, during the 1980–81 school year, revealed that every one of these students was referred because he had displayed behaviors in a regular classroom that were disruptive of normal classroom routines. Their teachers had initiated a referral process that would culminate in the child being labeled as severely emotionally disturbed and his being placed in a special education classroom with boys who had been similarly labeled.

Written reports by referring teachers often demonstrate a genuine concern for the child's welfare, as well as the teacher's growing frustration. In some of the cases, teachers felt that the child behaved in ways that made it impossible to operate the classroom. Meeting the needs of the "deviant" child meant, to some, sacrificing the needs of other students. The following note from a referring kindergarten teacher demonstrates a growing concern over Tyrone, the child described earlier in Dan Pallard's class. He and his older brother had recently moved to Lakeside and were placed in the custody of their aunt. Both boys are reported to have been living on the streets of another small northeastern city for almost three years. Tyrone was not quite five years old and his brother eight when they were found and taken into custody by the Social Services Department. He is one of the few children placed in the Education Center who all the staff at Evers considered to be "really disturbed."

> Tyrone was five in November, so you can realize that he is one of the youngest boys in our classroom. His height is small and he is solidly built. He has a real swagger when he walks and he always makes himself known at all costs. There is not a child in our classroom who is not scared of him because for no reason he will punch, jump on top of people, jump over people, kick. He does not have to be angered at all to have this happen. Some mornings everything seems beautifully peaceful and then he hits three or four people for no reason before he even sits down. There is hardly a moment of the morning that Mrs.

P. or I have to be aware of his whereabouts for the safety of the other children. I have been told by other mothers in the neighborhood that they almost had their boys shifted from our classroom at the very beginning of the year because they had witnessed his behavior in the neighborhood. I would have to say that in my 11 years of teaching I have never seen such an unpredictive [sic] child. Yes, he has also hit me for no good reason, yes, to get my attention. He will do anything to get that and he usually does because as I stated, I cannot ignore this. One morning he spread his shit all over the bathroom, and when Mrs. P. asked him why he did it, his answer was, "I like to do it." There is no special [music, art, gym] teacher in the building who wants him to come to their classroom. He usually stays with me and then because he is in a very small situation he can learn. Tyrone has a good keen mind. He adores stories, adores jungle gym, standing on his head, nursery rhymes, and has not missed one day of school. I want the best situation for this boy so I am calling on others for help and will abide by whatever decision we can come up with to help him be successful. We have had meetings with his aunt and she has stated that he and his brother practically brought themselves up for three years. Now we must help him.

This teacher, and most others referring children for special education services, believed that the child would receive the help he needed, once placed in a special class. However, this belief was not based on empirical evidence nor was it proven true in this study. Teachers continue to refer children for placement, and school districts, such as Lakeside, continue to place children in segregated special education classrooms. This process continues, not because it has been shown to benefit children like Tyrone but because it allows the regular classroom teacher to go on with the business of educating the "average" child in his or her classroom. Tyrone was clearly an emotionally needy child as were all of the children who had been placed in the Education Center. Their need for emotional support and a positive educational experience is not being questioned. Rather, the issue is whether or not these needs are symptomatic of a "sickness," as the label of severely emotionally disturbed implies, and whether or not their placement in a special education classroom meets their needs. The Education Center classes and programs that resemble it elsewhere certainly serve an important function within the educational system, i.e., they allow for the maintenance of the status quo while convincing the teacher and, usually, the child's parent(s), that the child is being helped. Mrs. Munroe put it this way: "Whatever exists is what people think these kids need."

When a teacher in the Lakeside school system wishes to refer a child to the Committee on the Handicapped, he or she is asked to file a report using the following format. The sample report in Figure 6.1 is on Clarence Johnson, one of the boys I came to know in the Education Center. It describes behaviors typically attributed to each of the Education Center students in their previous elementary school classrooms.

FIGURE 6.1
Sample Referral Report to the Committee on the Handicapped

Lakeside City School District — Department of Education for Children with Handicapping Conditions

Teacher's Report

Name: Johnson, Clarence
Birthdate: 3-19-71   **Age:** 8-3   **Date:** 6-14-79
Grade: 1 [His second year in first-grade] **Submitted by:** Mrs. Green
Reading level: 3 [Represents beginning first-grade reading skills.]
Math level: 3 [Represents beginning first-grade math skills.]
Subject area and grade: First
Academic ability and skills: Clarence when asked to do independent work either cries, says he doesn't know what you mean, doesn't know that, can't read it, etc. Under direct one-to-one will work.
Classroom behavior: Tears up papers. Carries on derogatory conversation with another child. Plays, gets out of seat, hits or kicks other children.

How well does the child handle:
1. Peer relationships: Not well — metes out his own justice.
2. Adult relationships (authority): Antagonistic and negative.
3. Transitions from one activity to another: [No teacher response]
4. Arrivals and Departures: Comes late, makes scene.
5. Following directions: Usually says "I don't know what you mean. You didn't tell me. I didn't hear you.

Helpful methods and/or materials used with child:
    Individual sheets (so task doesn't appear too big). Give close supervision because his chief need is attention and development of self-discipline.
School services currently provided: (i.e. Math lab, tutor, etc.) Resource.
Attendance: Good except March 18-30 when family problem. Almost always tardy to room from school breakfast (not often a late bus).
Attitude: Does not accept authority. Cannot bear correction. Destroys his work. Cries, throws furniture. In large group — jealous.

This report is accompanied by a behavorial rating scale provided by the school district. Teachers are asked to rate the child's behavior on a scale from one to five. The assumption being made in using this checklist is that it will provide an objective description of the child. The following directions are given to teachers as a guide:

1. Your own experiences with the child should be the only guide in rating. Ignore the opinions and comments of others.

2. Consider only the behavior of the child over the past month.
3. The child should be compared with the average youngster in a class-room setting . . . .
4. Do not try to interpret the student's hidden motives, feelings, or thoughts. Deal with your observations of the child's actual behavior.
5. Answer each question separately. Do not attempt to give answers which go together.
6. Rate items quickly. If undecided, continue to the next item and go back to it when you are done.
7. Do not hesitate to give high or low ratings. Avoid minimizing impressions by giving medium ratings. Extreme rating points are meant to be used whenever appropriate.
8. Rate all items. If it is impossible for you to answer an item due to lack of opportunity to observe, circle that item.

These directions clearly ask the impossible. Few, if any teachers come to the point of filling out this scale without having already decided that the child being referred belongs in someone else's class. She has talked to other teachers about the child in question. The opinions of colleagues exert a powerful influence that a teacher cannot ignore, despite of the directions given on the behavior rating scale. Once a teacher has the "average" child in mind as a basis of comparison, the behavior of the deviant child is no longer the only consideration given when rating his behavior. The teacher's thoughts move back and forth between the behavior she has seen displayed by the child under consideration and her idealized image of the typical child. This process is itself interpretive, regardless of the direction given.

The specific questions asked of classroom teachers on this rating scale pertain to the child's social behavior in the classroom. The teacher is asked, "Compared to the average child, how often does this student . . . ?" Most are examples of negative behaviors, such as "Act defiant (i.e., will not do what he is asked to do, says: 'I won't do it')"; "Poke, torment or tease classmates"; "Criticize the ideas, suggestions or work of peers?" These three items present excellent examples of some of the behaviors on this scale that are subject to a great deal of variation with regard to the meaning they may have, both for the child being described and for the teacher observing the behavior. To the Black child, they may be behaviors that are meant to enhance status among his peers. To the White middle-class teacher, this behavior, when compared to that of his or her *average* child, is not only disruptive, but also may be frightening. Interpretations of children's behaviors are shared between teachers in the teachers' lounge, are reinforced by psychiatric and educational definitions of emotional disturbance and will later be sanctified by the Committee on the Handicapped.

The teacher's report and behavioral checklist will next be brought before the school building's Pupil Services Team. This team meets regularly in each school building in Lakeside to discuss children who are experiencing difficulty. The Pupil Services Team usually consists of the school principal, psychologist, a special education teacher, social worker (there are school social workers only in those buildings with a large percentage of children with low-income families), nurse, and other school personnel connected with remedial and support services, such as a special education resource teacher or instructional specialist. If the team decides that a child needs special education services, it changes its hat and becomes the school building's Committee on the Handicapped. In this way, it is argued, the committee will know the child well and will have first tried altering the regular school program before taking the step of labeling the child as handicapped. The parent of a handicapped child from that school building's attendance area and the school physician, both mandated members of the Committee on the Handicapped, are missing from the Pupil Services Team. These members will be invited to attend meetings when these become official C.O.H. sessions.

The response of the Pupil Services Team to the teacher's referral varies greatly from school to school. At Evers, there is rarely a consideration given for special education placement other than for the services of the special education resource teacher. The school social worker would contact the family directly and get to know the child. The psychologist often observes the child in the referring classroom and perhaps assess the child's skills and deficits on an individual basis. The team would then reconvene with specific suggestions for the classroom teacher.

At other schools, a teacher's referral of a child would be followed by a letter to the parents indicating that the Pupil Services Team would like to have the child evaluated. The following is a copy of the form letter developed by the Lakeside school district to tell parents of the school's concerns and to secure parental permission to test the child. The letter follows a format that is in strict compliance with state regulations. This does not, however, guarantee that parents either know what is going on with their child in school or understand the possible ramifications of the assessment that will follow.

The following note, haltingly printed originally by Mrs. Evans, a parent of a boy in the Education Center to this child's teacher, demonstrates this woman's limited literacy. Certainly, the letter from the Pupil Personnel Team had little meaning to her:

I am write few line to
let you no will tell Mr. B.

> Then that i wat to
> see him above is Andre i
> have.
>   reivee Letter from Hosptil
> St. Vinsente for Andre ene come
>   over let wont to do i will
> Be home round 11:30 all day
>   Miss E.

Like each of the other parents whose child had been labeled severely emotionally disturbed, Mrs. Evans had received a letter from a Pupil Services Team. Many parents do not respond to these letters, either because, like Mrs. Evans, they cannot read very well, may not open "official-looking" mail, are confused, or are possibly overwhelmed by other circumstances in their lives. There are certainly some parents who have no interest in relating to school and possibly some who "just don't care about their kids" (this last explanation is the one most frequently given by Lakeside school personnel for parents' unresponsive behavior). Regulations now de-

---

FIGURE 6.2

Dear Parent or Guardian:

The _____ School Pupil Services team would like to evaluate your child. This evaluation will include one or more of the following areas: achievement levels, classroom observation, intellectual level, interview by psychologist and/or psychiatrist, personality and perceptual motor development.

The School Pupil Services team requesting this evaluation includes the principal as chairman, the school social worker or guidance counselor, the school nurse, the school psychologist, a parent and one or more teachers. The team will use the evaluationinformation to plan an appropriate program for your child.

The results of this evaluation are available to you. Please call the school if you wish a conference.

Your written permission is required before we may evaluate your child. Please complete the form below and return it to school by _____.
date

Sincerely,

Principal

Please mark (x one):
_____ I hereby give permission
_____ I hereby refuse permission
to have my child _____, grade _____ evaluated.
            name of child

_____.
            Signature of parent or guardian   date

---

mand, however, that schools and parents communicate with each other, if only to get a parent's signature for permission to test his or her child.

Once parental permission has been secured, the school psychologist will see the child individually and administer standardized tests of achievement, intelligence, and perceptual motor functioning, and evaluate the child's personality through informal observation and projective tests. Although the standardized assessment devices used in the majority of American public schools have been demonstrated to have strong cultural biases that result in the underestimation of the minority child's potential (Hobbs, 1976; Mercer, 1973; Salvia & Ysseldyke, 1978), and the validity and reliability of projective devices are questionable (O'Leary, 1972), both continue to be used as the primary means of evaluating children in American public schools.

The evaluation presented in Figure 6.3 is an example of what is considered to be a complete psychological evaluation of Robert Phillips, a child being considered for special education placement. The conclusions drawn by the evaluator are based on the definitions given to Robert's behavior. Psychologists often rely on "clinical judgments" in offering diagnoses. In this case, however, one is left with the impression that the conclusions and recommendations given in this report are based solely on objectively determined criteria, and that the evaluator believes, based on the child's behavior and performance during the testing sessions, that this child is emotionally disturbed.

The recommendations made in this evaluation focus on trying to fix the child by offering interventions outside of the regular education structure. There were no suggestions made for alternative instructional approaches or behavior management within the regular classroom. Rather, because he

---

FIGURE 6.3

Sample Psychological Evaluation

Name: Robert Phillips
Date: 12–19–78
Birth: 6–30–70
Age: 8–6
Grade: 1st, repeating; Calhoun School

Tests: Wechsler Intelligence Scale for Children — Revised; Human Figure Drawing.

Referral: Robert has attended this school for two weeks and was referred by the school principal because he repeated K. and is now repeating first grade and some educational planning is therefore necessary. Robert entered foster care this year and is now in his second foster home.

Test Results: On the WISC-R Robert acheived a Verbal IQ of 75, a Performance IQ of 81, and a Full Scale IQ of 76. This places Robert within the "borderline" range of intelligence according to the Wechsler norms. Considering his past academic failures this seems to be the level at which Robert generally functions. *However,* there are indications that Robert's potential is higher than this. On three subtests Robert scored at his age level and on three more subtests he scored slightly below his age level. Robert quickly understood each task and his task analysis skills were very good. Robert's spontaneous vocabulary and language patterns are adequately developed for his age.

On the Verbal Scale Robert did well on Vocabulary and Conprehension. He had a lot of difficulty with Information, Arithmetic, and Similarities. He showed a tendency to perseverate from one question to the next. Several of his answers were unusual and unnecessarily related to violence.

On the Performance Scale Robert scored in the average range on most subtests. He had some difficulty with Object Assembly and extreme difficulty with Block Designs. Robert is confused by tasks requiring spatial relations. This problem in Robert extends to his reading where he also makes reversals (he read "on" for "no").

On the Human Figure Drawing Robert scored at the "low average" level for his age. His drawing included some details (eyelashes, waist) but omitted more necessary items (feet, nose). Robert seems to have some skills in expressing himself through drawings.

Observations: Robert was very cooperative and he enjoyed the test items and the attention. He gets very silly but in a one-to-one situation it is easy to get him back on task. Robert is quite active and he is usually in motion, his hands are never still. When Robert has a task that requires him to use his hands, it seems to help him focus his attention and to limit some of his randon movement.

Robert's self-image ranges from weak to negative. He has difficulty controlling his own behavior. He is very willing to talk and volunteer information about family problems (father's drinking, brother's breaking into a car, his placement in a foster home). He needs an adult to help him sort out the many things that he has experienced.

Summary and Recommendations: Robert's academic progress is limited by emotional factors and below average intelligence. Although his WISC-R IQ falls at the upper limit of the EMR range there is evidence that his potential is higher. However, his emotional problems are significant and may continue to interfere with his school performance. Robert's primary problem is his emotional disturbance, and educational planning must take this into consideration. The following options could be considered by ther Calhoun COH:

1. Refer to Dr. Flagg [district psychiatrist] for placement.
2. Include in Calhoun Resource Program for "emotional reasons" and focus on counseling and behavior.
3. Refer to ED subcommittee for placement in ED class.
4. Refer to EMR class and hope that his teacher there could meet his *great* emotional *needs.*

Susan Placer
School Psychologist

has not conformed to the norms of behavior established both for the testing situation and for the classroom, Robert is perceived as "sick." The first recommendation, that he see the school district's psychiatrist would further reinforce this perspective. Dr. Flagg's belief in the pathology inherent in the single-parent, female-headed Black family has predisposed him to perceive Black boys raised by single mothers as emotionally disturbed.

Disturbed or Disturbing?

In Lakeside, in order for any child to be designated as either emotionally disturbed or severely emotionally disturbed he or she must first be evaluated by Dr. Flagg. It is not mandated by education laws that a psychiatrist corroborate an educational diagnosis of emotional disturbance. However, it has become an entrenched tradition in the Lakeside school district. It has also served to legitimize the practice of assigning this label to children who are disruptive in school.

Dr. Flagg follows a medical model of explaining deviant behavior and leans heavily on a deterministic and sexually oriented perspective that is often associated with psychoanalysis.

Question: How would you characterize the theoretical position you follow?

Dr. Flagg: I attempt a synthesis of the social-traditional and the molecular-biological. You know that people are exotic creatures with an awesome potential. They also have the potential to do terrible danger. There is an animal right underneath all of us. . . . You know, these cute little kids are really narcissistic. All they really are interested in is themselves and all they are interested in really is also sex. You know, the White teacher sees that and gets really upset. They are always exposing themselves. You catch them pulling down little girls' pants. And what can you expect? It's a model from their father.

There have been voices in both the community and the school system that have begun to speak up against such interpretations of children's behavior as evidence of their pathology. Mrs. Henty, a Black grandmother whose children went to Evers, is outspoken about what she believes to be the misinterpretation of Black children's behaviors by White school officials. She explained the Black child's openness with his sexuality from quite a different perspective from that of Dr. Flagg:

Our kids are taught to stand up for themselves and be proud. This kind of aggressiveness and self-identity is taught now in the pre-K. And that's good, but when the kid hits third and fourth grade and starts using it, then he gets labeled as emotionally disturbed and crazy.

> When our kids feel proud, they have learned to show it by standin' with hands on hips, and stickin' out their chest and body. The teacher sees this and says he is trying to show his penis. Another thing is that we are very physical with our kids and show our affection this way. Kids are always touchin' and strokin'. Well, the little Black boy likes his teacher and climbs up on her lap and touches her breast. Well, oh my. . . . The teacher says, "He *knows* what he was doing."

This woman's perspective includes the expectation of White professional stereotyping of Blacks as sex-crazed and, consequently, the belief that Black student behavior will be misinterpreted. As she put it, "White folks think we always wind up in the bedroom."

Dr. Flagg does not see the child's behavior from within the context of the child's experiences. Nor does he attempt to explore alternative definitions of the child's behavior with their families. He has a fixed conceptualization regarding the behaviors and motives of children who come to be identified as emotionally disturbed:

> There is a pattern if you look at these kids. They're always in trouble. . . . Motivation is lacking. These kids are not willing to sacrifice their pleasure for what's required for learning. They are not able to say to themselves, "Hey, look, I don't want to sit in this chair, but I'm going to learn this, these words or these arithmetic problems."

Emotionally disturbed children are differentiated from those he identifies as mentally retarded if their tested I.Q.'s are "not way down in the sixties," but still "don't fit into the class." Their lack of fit is evidence of their deviancy and not, as would be proposed from an ecological perspective, evidence of a mismatch between the demands and expectations of the system and that of the child. The goal of an ecologically based assessment would not be to arrive at a diagnosis, as is the case here, but rather to develop a profile of the child that would identify the points of discordance between the child and the environments in which he interacts.

Following a medical model, Dr. Flagg's primary responsibility is diagnostic. He is responsible for determining whether or not a child is disturbed and the severity of that disturbance. In most cases, the referring school presents its choice of diagnosis to the psychiatrist, based on whether the child can be kept in a regular classroom and be supported by a special education resource teacher or if the referring school believes that the child is too disruptive of normal classroom procedures. If the latter is the case, then it will be recommended that the child be placed in a self-contained, segregated classroom for the severely emotionally disturbed. Dr. Flagg makes the final determination regarding the severity of the child's disorder, using the following "evaluation procedure":

I have the kid in my office and I provoke him. I set him up. I shift to a critical, admonishing tone from a really pleasant tone. You know, I start out nice with the kid and friendly and warm and then I shift. And then when my tone shifts, I look for clues in the kid. I look for the clenched fist, the flushed face, the blood pressure rising. The anxiety is rising in the kid. The kid that throws over a chair and runs out of the room when I start to put pressure on him, he's an S.E.D. I shift my tone and I look for behavioral manifestations of anxiety. Sometimes what I do is I'll sit and play ball with the kid, nice and friendly. Then, suddenly, I'll take it and I'll throw it at the kid's face. Right in his face, and I'll see how he reacts. If the kid looks at it as, well, "This is a ball in the face game," and he throws it back at me in a playful kind of way, that's not an emotionally disturbed kid. I bring a kid up to violence and see how he's going to react. And also I never see a kid alone. There are other people, so it's not just me he's interacting with. It's also how does he deal with other people seeing him, the whole interaction. I can tell. If you generally like a kid and can identify with him, you can sort of see that the kid is okay.

By the time the boys from the Education Center reached Dr. Flagg's office, they had encountered a good many other interactions in their class-rooms and throughout their school experience that had reinforced the type of behavior that would be defined by the doctor as evidence of disturbance. An understanding of this phenomenon was described by many: the Evers teachers, parents, principals, Blacks who have lived in Lakeside for many years, and by teachers at other elementary schools who were identified as being successful in their management and teaching of Black children who had been labeled as emotionally disturbed. Most agreed that initially, upon entering school, most Black male children were probably no more ag-gressive than any other boys, but through their interactions with teachers (primarily, but not always, White females), their aggressive behavior in-creased.

Dr. Flagg's definition of these children's behavior is, however, the official and sanctioned definition. His perspective and the power attached to his professional identity allow the school district to remove difficult-to-manage children from classrooms without having to question any prior assump-tions about how these classrooms are being operated. The director of pupil services for the Lakeside city schools, Mr. Gould, a White, middle-aged clinically trained psychologist, supports Dr. Flagg's position. He is respon-sible for the supervision of psychological and support services other than those provided by the Special Education Department in this district. His orientation sets the tone for how assessments are carried out and what support services are considered appropriate for nonhandicapped students. Mr. Gould recognizes that although some of the behaviors exhibited by children who are labeled as disturbed may be somewhat appropriate in other environments that the child experiences, the same behaviors when

seen in school are inappropriate and therefore are symptoms of disturbance. Mr. Gould elaborates:

> If a kid is violent in an appropriate place then he is not "emotionally dis-
> turbed." I understand that. If he is on the street and he has to be violent to
> survive, that is not "emotional disturbance." But when he is violent in an
> inappropriate place, when he brings that kind of outburst into the school,
> then that's an example of inappropriate behavior. The kid has to learn to play
> the game and how to survive in a variety of settings.

Mr. Gould believes that there is a greater prevalence of emotional disturbance among Black children both because of their "subculture," which he
believes is dominated by violence, and because of their home lives. The
disturbed child will usually come from a home with a very young, unwed
mother who lacks good parenting skills. These homes, he believes, are
often disorganized and, as a result, the children raised in them do not
develop the "basic trust" that Erikson (1963) has identified as being necessary for healthy emotional development.

In spite of the belief that the child's misbehavior in school is the result of
pathological child rearing, the Lakeside school system offers little if any
supportive interventions to the families of children labeled as severely
emotionally disturbed. The child's life outside of school may be explored as
part of the assessment process. The purpose of gathering a social history is
not, however, to offer services or support to the child's family or community, but rather to gather more data to base a diagnosis on. In Robert's
case, it was found that he had been placed in two foster homes in the six
months prior to his coming to school in Lakeside. He and his younger
brother had lived with his mother in a small town nearby. They had moved
frequently, changing schools three times, to avoid both their landlord and
their alcoholic and abusive father. Robert's mother eventually placed both
boys in foster care, but since there were no Black families in their community who would take these children, they were sent to Lakeside. Their
first foster home found both children to be unmanageable, and so, after
several months, the brothers were separated. Robert had just been placed,
without his brother, in his new foster home when he entered this school.
Two weeks later, he was referred to the Pupil Services Team.

Nothing written into Robert's records indicates that his behavior was
viewed as a normal reaction to the stressful situation he had just experienced and that there necessarily would be a difficult period of adjustment
for this child. Rather, because his behavior did not fit the expectations of
school personnel regarding appropriate school behavior, he was referred for
special education services. No interventions are suggested for Robert's life
outside of school or for his mother or brother. This is not seen as the

jurisdiction or purview of the school system, but rather as being the "business" of other human service agencies. Collaboration or consultation with these agencies is not suggested. Instead, the school believes Robert is the only problem it has to deal with—his behavior and learning in the school setting. The school certainly recognized that Robert's life outside of school affected his school performance. However, this information was not used as the basis of providing supports to those other external systems, but rather as further corroboration of the child's emotional disorder.

When all data are gathered on a child, i.e., his health history, social history, teacher's report, behavioral checklist and psychological evaluation, a formal meeting is called by the school's Committee on the Handicapped. The child's parent is invited to attend and to listen to the evidence presented. Parents are asked for their opinions but, in the case of the children who came to be labeled as severely emotionally disturbed, few feel they have much to add. They are told their child will be helped by placement in a smaller class, where he will receive more individual attention. Rarely have the parents of Education Center children objected to this type of placement.

The recommendations made by the psychologist who evaluated Robert in addition to the recommendation that he see Dr. Flagg, did not offer any additional insights into the child's educational needs. It seems, rather, that the psychologist assumes that saying a child has "emotional needs" or that he should receive services for "emotional reasons" would somehow be translated into concrete, individualized services. In reality, these statements contribute very little toward understanding this child, how he sees the world, his strengths, weaknesses, hopes, fears and desires. There is also no suggestion that Robert's learning deficits, distractibility, constant motor activity, and difficulty with spatial relations are interrelated with each other and with his problem behaviors in class. This kind of focus might have led to a diagnosis of a learning disability rather than an emotional disturbance. However, the expectation in Lakeside that Black children from single-parent, low-income families will have severe emotional problems may have precluded a learning disabled label.

It is assumed that children with learning disabilities misbehave in school because of their frustration with academic tasks. These students are considered to be intellectually average or above average. It is also assumed that they do not have underlying "psychopathology." In Lakeside, if a White child from a middle-class, two-parent family performed in the same way as did Robert on an individually administered psychological evaluation, it is likely that he would have been labeled as learning disabled. The child would have remained in a regular classroom and would receive supportive services from a special education resource teacher. Even though Robert could have been labeled as L.D., this would not happen, both because of the assumptions of school officials and because Robert's teacher and building principal wanted him removed from his classroom and placed elsewhere. Since the only children placed in self-contained classrooms at that time were those labeled as educable mentally retarded or as severely emotionally disturbed, these would be the only labels considered.

Given Robert's history and low average tested I.Q., it is not surprising that Dr. Flagg labeled this child as severely emotionally disturbed. After seeing the psychiatrist, there would still be several small steps to complete before the child would be placed in Evers' Education Center or any of the other programs for severely emotionally disturbed children in Lakeside. After Dr. Flagg confirms the diagnosis, the school district's Subcommittee on Emotional Disturbance of its Committee on the Handicapped will discuss the case, and usually, according to Mrs. Munroe, "rubber-stamp" the label and placement recommendations made by the school C.O.H. Parents and other interested professionals are invited to this meeting by an official letter. Few parents ever appear. Only in the rare instance, when a parent has objected to his or her child's placement, has a parent attended.

Once the decision is finalized, another official letter, such as the following, is sent to the child's family. In reading this letter, consider the young, poorly educated single mothers who received similar letters. Here the parent is not told that the child has been labeled as severely emotionally disturbed, but only that the child is being placed in a special education for "emotional reasons."

Obviously, more than the child's emotions made this placement necessary. The emotional response of those with whom he interacted also played a large part in this decision, but is never officially recognized. The child would now be placed in a situation where all his classmates would have gone through the same process of having failed to meet the expectations of a regular classroom setting. If the child was placed in the program at Evers for severely emotionally disturbed students, then there would be the possibility that he would have the opportunity to interact with other students from the rest of the school because of its mainstreaming program. This could happen at Evers because most of the labeled children were not perceived as all that different from the typical Evers student by the Evers staff. Mary Flynn put it this way, talking about Carl Smith, a child from the Education Center who had been mainstreamed into her second-grade classroom and who will be discussed in the following chapter:

> I've got a lot of kids that I think, if they were in another school, would be in an Education Center type situation. He's all right in this room. I think if you took Carl and put him in a very middle class school, he'd freak them right out. I'm just a lot more used to that. In this class I've got 22 kids and there are

Re: Notice of Recommendation
for Special Education
Services

July 23, 1979

Mrs. Andra Evans
154 North Avenue
Lakeside

Dear Mrs. Evans:

The Committee on the Handicapped believes that your child, Andre Evans, possesses a handicapping condition to a degree sufficient to warrant provision of special education services, and recommends that Andre be assigned to the S.E.D. Class at Evers School. This placement is necessary because of emotional reasons. This recommendation is based on school reports, psychological evaluation, Wechsler Intelligence Scale for Children Test, Bender Gestalt Test, House-Tree-Person Test.

All school files, records and reports pertaining to your child will be available for your inspection, interpretation and review. You may duplicate such records at reasonable costs.

If you object to the proposed action, you may request, in writing, within 10 days of receipt of this notice, an impartial hearing with the Superintendent of Schools pursuant to subdivision (b) of Section 100.20 of the Regulations of the Commissioner of Education, a copy of which is enclosed.

If you are still dissatisfied, you may initiate an appeal from the decision of the Superintendent. Within 10 days of the receipt of the final determination sought to be reviewed, your appeal shall be directed, in writing, to the Commissioner of Education, who shall decide the appeal solely upon the record in the proceedings before the Superintendent. However, you may submit statements in support of or opposition to the determination sought to be reviewed. The decision of the Superintendent shall be affirmed if supported by substantial evidence.

In the event of a hearing your child may remain in his present educational placement pending a determination by the Superintendent or an appeal from the Superintendent's decision to the Commissioner of Education if an appeal is taken to him, unless your child's presence in that program poses a continuing danger to persons or property, or threatens disruption of the academic process.

You may obtain an independent evaluation of your child.

Very truly yours,

Carolyn Smedley

Acting Supervisor, Special Education Division

---

probably six or seven others that I am constantly aware of, what they're thinking and what they're doing. And he would be one of those, but no more so than six or seven others. . . . I don't know that if Carl was at Evers he would have ended up in the Education Center. He was at another school.

The ways that teachers at Evers interact with their students are recognized as qualitatively different from those of the majority of teachers at other elementary schools in Lakeside by Evers' teachers themselves, and by other school personnel who have had extensive experience in schools throughout the city. These include psychologists, social workers, principals, an itinerant reading teacher, an assistant superintendent, and even Dr. Flagg, who made the following remarks while addressing the Ever's Committee on the Handicapped:

> You people are unique. You do a wonderful job. The problem is getting these kids used to the atmosphere out there. It's like you create a breed of hot-house flowers. You nurture these kids and they grow and blossom. Then we take them from this nice, warm temperature and put them into a twenty degree below zero environment and they're destroyed.

7

Two Children Labeled "Severely Emotionally Disturbed"

Examining the careers of two of the children who were placed in the Education Center can best demonstrate the impact of the events described in earlier chapters of this book. The process they experienced from their entry into the Lakeside school system through their placement in the Education Center, and, in Carl Smith's case, out again, will be illustrated. The details of each Education Center child's experiences are certainly unique. Neither Michael Thomas nor Carl Smith represent all the students who have been placed at Evers or in similar programs throughout the United States. Rather, they are presented as examples of how children become caught up in the politics of the grown-up world. Their having been labeled as severely emotionally disturbed has had a significant impact on their lives. Unfortunately, in spite of the intent of P.L. 94–142, this influence has not always been a positive one.

Michael Thomas

Michael Thomas was introduced earlier in the discussion of the Education Center. He was the child who was punished by his teacher, Barbara Sheppard, and humiliated by Laurie, the Education Center's social worker. He began his school career at age four and a half in a neighborhood pre-school program. His mother reported that she was unaware of any problems there, or in his kindergarten class at the Frankfurt School, a predominantly Black school in the neighborhood adjacent to Evers. In December 1976, Mrs. Thomas transferred Michael into kindergarten at the Carey School, a predominantly White elementary school, where she felt he would get a better education. Carey had not had any Black students prior to 1965, drawing its student body from its White, ethnic, working-class neighborhood. By 1975, nine percent of its students were Black. In 1977, under the impetus of the city's Alternative Attendance Program, it had a Black student enrollment of 21 percent. Michael was one of these students.

White people's behavior was as foreign to Michael as his behavior was to his teachers and classmates. Living in the public housing projects had given him little opportunity for contact with Whites before coming to this school. Apparently, their rules were somewhat different from those at home. In school, the children were "asked" to do things, whereas in the Thomas' home, the children were "told" what to do. In school, there did not seem to be any consequences for not following directions, whereas at home you might get "whooped" or lose privileges. In fact, for large segments of the school day, no one told you directly what to do. The teacher assumed the children knew the rules.

Michael's behavior became problematic to his kindergarten teacher at Carey within a few months. He did not seem to know how to play appropriately or how to follow basic classroom procedures. A referral was made to the school psychologist, who filed the following report (statements written in parenthesis are the psychologist's interpretations):

Psychological Report

Reason for Referral: Behavioral Problems.
Techniques Use: Observation of classroom.
Observations: Michael is a boy who transferred from Frankfurt after school began
  this fall. He seems to be an active child who is out of his seat quite often
  (Refusing to persist at a given task—the one exception noted was eating, in
  which he attended to the task for three to four minutes without speaking out
  of turn or disrupting the class in any way). He offered to share some of his
  snack with a friend (a positive sign), but in order to do so, he broke one of the
  class rules (a negative sign). He is a leader who draws attention to himself in
  both positive (one boy was proud of his work with clay, and wanted Michael
  to approve), as well as negative means (i.e., instead of waiting for Miss K. to
  come to him to approve his work, Michael took it upon himself to go wash his
  hands, talking and playing with others along the way). He did not ask permission once in the one and one half hours I have seen him.

Clearly, from this report, none of Michael's behaviors were threatening to the physical well-being of the class. They are obviously the behavior of a child who is interested in his peers, wanting to impress and share what he has with them. The examiner, however, has interpreted and evaluated this child's behavior from a perspective that does not take the child's point of view into account. Rather, some behaviors are judged, by the examiner's standards, as being examples of either positive or negative behavior. Michael's getting out of his seat, for example, is defined as "refusing to persist at a given task," rather than being seen as a possible example of his motivation to explore the materials in the room or interest in interacting

with those White-skinned children with whom he has ne
opportunity to play.

It is important to keep in mind that Michael had pre
nursery school and a kindergarten classroom in Black school
income neighborhood. In the Carey kindergarten, you were expected to
know that you had to wait for the teacher to come to your seat before you
got up to play. In his other schools, children were either told what they
could or couldn't do, or allowed to play freely. Children did not ask permission there. They waited to be told what to do. If they were not told that they
could not do something, then they assumed they could do it. If they did
something they were not supposed to do, they got "whooped." In the kindergarten classroom at Carey, there did not appear to be any consequences
for doing whatever one wanted to do, except that the teacher sometimes
yelled.

No specific suggestions were made to Michael's teacher at the end of this
report. Instead, the psychologist decided that he needed to speak with
Michael's parents. A lack of awareness of this child's life outside of school is
apparent from the concluding remarks written on this report: "A letter
went home inviting Michael's parents to see me, but no response was
forthcoming." The psychologist was unaware that Michael lived in a single-
parent family, and had no knowledge of the other circumstances of this
child's life. The following information was gathered the following Fall on
"Family Composition" for the school social worker's report to be presented
to the school's Committee on the Handicapped as documentation of
Michael's emotional disturbance:

Family Composition

Mother: Bertha Thomas was born on May 3, 1950, in Birmingham, Alabama. She
attended schools in Birmingham and completed tenth grade. She is employed
at the General Hospital in the Dietary Department.

Mrs. Thomas is a soft-spoken woman who seems interested in her children
and one who has been cooperative in planning what is best for Michael. She
feels she has a good relationship with both her children. Her concern about
Michael centers around his reluctance to speak out about his feelings. She
indicated she never has problems with Michael. He has been good in his
behavior around home and children in the neighborhood. She feels that he
accepts discipline well, and usually denies him T.V. and other things when he
misbehaves. There are times, however, after being disciplined he continues to
misbehave and "tries to get even."

Natural Father: Robert Thomas, birthdate October 15, 1945.

According to Mrs. Thomas, she separated from her husband when Michael
was an infant. He has never seen him since. There is no contact with the

natural father. According to Mrs. Thomas, her boyfriend, whom she plans to marry, has been considered by Michael as his father. Michael is aware of the fact that he is not his natural father.
This man is presently serving time in prison for burglary. He is to be paroled in June, 1977. Mrs. Thomas has visited him with her children. She states that he loves children and he and Michael have a good relationship.

Siblings: May Thompson, birthdate May 17, 1972. May was born out of wedlock and given the legal name of Thompson. Her natural father lives in Lakeside. Up to the age of two years, he visited his daughter quite regularly. He now sees her occasionally.

This information, if considered in understanding Michael's school behavior, might have provided a framework for working with this child and his mother, rather than immediately placing him in a special education program. Instead, Michael's family background would be seen as the cause of his misbehavior and "disturbance." The loyalties that this boy may have had for his imprisoned stepfather and the lessons he had learned about the world from his experiences were ignored. The following psychological evaluation, completed soon after Michael entered first grade, again illustrates the way in which behavior is described from the perspective of the examiner rather than from one that attempts to understand the meaning an experience may have for the child.

Psychological Evaluation

Reason for Referral: Michael was referred by his teacher, Mrs. P., because of his disruptive classroom behavior. He finds it difficult to get along with other children and gets into many fights. Michael is easily distracted and is unable to concentrate on one task for a long period of time.

Classroom Observations: Michael was observed during an unstructured activity. Throughout the observation period, Michael would get out of his seat and crawl on the floor. When he was seated, he occasionally pounded his desk with his fist or played with some papers and paid little attention to the coloring activity and made little progress with his drawing.

Testing Observations: Michael was very willing to come with the psychologist. However, once Michael entered the testing situation, and he realized what would be expected of him, his enthusiasm diminished. Michael seemed fairly interested in the first few (W.P.P.S.I.) subtests presented to him. However, as the testing continued, Michael became less interested, gave up easily and wanted to return to his classroom. Throughout the examination Michael was extremely concerned over what the psychologist was writing down. When the psychologist jotted down any extra notes along the margins, Michael stopped working and demanded to know the contents of the notes. He also became alarmed when he discovered that the psychologist had a folder with his name on it.

Michael's apparent concern with the psychologist's behavior is presented in this report in such a way that it can be interpreted as evidence of disturbance, more specifically paranoia. Not knowing that Michael had visited his stepfather in prison, as well as not taking into account the child's numerous contacts with White social service and educational officials carrying folders, neglects information that is vital to understanding the meaning of this child's behavior.

This psychological evaluation continues with a description of the results of the psychometric tests that were administered. A Verbal I.Q. of 90, Performance I.Q. of 88, and Full Scale I.Q. of 89 are interpreted as evidence of "dull normal" intellectual functioning. The well-documented influence of cultural bias on I.Q. scores is not taken into account. The fact that Michael was not wearing the eyeglasses that had been prescribed for him (he lost them earlier, it is noted in another report) is also not offered as a possible explanation for his poor performance on either the Wechsler Pre-School and Primary Scales of Intelligence (W.P.P.S.I.), the Bender-Gestalt, or the House-Tree-Person tests, which rely on adequate visual-motor performance by the child. Instead, his inadequate drawings are used as further evidence of his illness, in spite of the known lack of validity of these types of projective devices. The psychologist interpreted Michael's drawings of a house, tree and person in the following way:

> Michael's drawings suggest that he is a child who is not apt to open up and really explore his feelings and ideas to others. His drawings also suggest that he has aggressive, acting-out tendencies.

The written recommendations that followed did not offer suggestions to the classroom teacher or parent in terms of management or teaching strategies. Rather, they recommended a "small group situation" operated under a "token reinforcement program," thus laying the groundwork for Michael's placement in a self-contained special education class. The forwarding of these reports to Dr. Flagg, and the psychiatrist's subsequent meeting with this child, were all that were needed to complete an official diagnosis.

In this child's case, the label would result in his placement at the Clearview Children's School, a privately operated school and day-treatment center for young severely emotionally disturbed children. It is not clear from the records, nor from anyone with whom I spoke, why Michael was sent to Clearview instead of being initially referred to the Education Center. In

January 1978, a psychological evaluation was conducted at the Clearview Children's School in order to determine if this was an appropriate placement. A Clearview psychologist concluded his report with the following statement: "At the present time, he does not appear to be seriously emotionally disturbed, but his efforts at self-control need to be supported and encouraged to reduce the possibility of serious aggressive acting-out in the future." He recommended that Michael be placed in a public school program for behaviorally disordered children.

The Clearview psychologist described Michael's attempts first to manipulate by guile and then, when they failed, to get his way through intimidation:

> As we spent more time together, and Michael became more familiar with me, his initial cooperativeness diminished. He gradually began to test my limits, primarily for the purpose of leaving the test situation. He began with very subtle requests such as offering to take a pencil to a secretary outside or getting up without saying anything and simply putting on his jacket. When these efforts failed, he became more direct in asking if we could stop now and go over to the gym instead. Although he did not show any angry feelings toward me when I denied his request, he did pretend to throw my pencil out of the window as an indirect way of getting back at me.

This examiner defined this behavior as "testing the limits" of the situation, not as evidence of disturbance. Apparently, the public school officials, including Dr. Flagg, saw things differently. Perhaps Dr. Flagg's evaluation did not go as smoothly as did the one at Clearview. It is quite possible that Michael did not appreciate Dr. Flagg's "ball in the face game," for he was soon labeled as severely emotionally disturbed and placed, in the Fall of 1978, at Clearview.

None of the teacher reports nor any of the psychological or psychiatric reports written during the year and a half Michael spent at Clearview indicate that the staff believed him to be seriously disturbed. Within six months of his placement, the Clearview staff recommended to the school district Committee on the Handicapped that Michael be returned to a public school. Almost another full year passed before this was actually done.

The Clearview staff felt strongly that Michael should not be returned to the school that had initially referred him. Notes from a staff meeting there indicate that another school was felt to more appropriate: "Some of Michael's problems dealing with school had to do with being in an environment that he had difficulty relating to." The following "Recommendations for Placement," written by his classroom teacher at Clearview, seems to describe the environment that could be found at Evers:

Michael will need a structured classroom and activities (though not necessarily traditional). Firm limitations would need to be stated, as well as clear expectations. Adults involved with Michael in a school setting would need to establish a warm and trusting relationship. Praise and humor would be successful techniques. Grouping with peers from a comparative socio-economic background would be recommended. While Michael is appropriately friendly and outgoing, he is a good candidate for modeling of peers (i.e., of positive and/or negative behavior).

Although the District Committee on the Handicapped agreed to place Michael in a regular classroom at Evers, with Resource Room assistance, the Evers Committee on the Handicapped rejected the idea of placing Michael directly into a regular classroom. Members of Evers' staff who had been a part of that decision explained that because Michael had spent a year and a half at Clearview, he certainly must have been more disturbed initially than children who were referred directly to the Education Center. If he was better, that was seen to indicate that he was better than the other children at Clearview, and not necessarily better than the children in the Education Center. The staff at Evers felt he needed to be placed in the Education Center first, so that they could get a chance to observe his behavior in this environment. Only after they considered him to be ready would he be recommended to be mainstreamed into the rest of the school.

The Evers staff, who as a group were sensitive to the misuse and abuse of labels, particularly as they are attached to minority children, fell prey to the powerful biasing effects of psychiatric labels. Michael's prior placement in a psychiatric facility which was known as a placement site for "really disturbed" children multiplied this effect. Previous records were overlooked, as was the recommendation that Michael be placed in an environment where he would have the opportunity to observe positive peer behavior models. At eight years of age, Michael had not yet had the opportunity to interact in school with other children who could facilitate his development. Instead, he had spent his first year and a half in a public school building where neither the adults nor the children related to him, and his next year and a half in an environment where most of the children were psychotic and autistic-like and could barely relate to anyone.

In September 1979, Michael was placed in the Education Center. The classroom he entered is described as having been wild. The teacher was unable to control or manage her students, and, needless to say, little if any academic work was achieved. She resigned in January 1980, and was replaced by Barbara Sheppard, who had little experience in managing this type of classroom. As seen earlier, Barbara's classroom was not much better than her predecessor's. Michael was given little opportunity there to learn appropriate behavior, either through direct instruction or through peer modeling. In fact, the very behaviors that had gotten him in trouble in the first place were being continually reinforced.

Despite the lack of opportunities presented in school and his continual confrontations with Barbara Sheppard, Michael demonstrated that he could get along with the other children and teachers and progress at academic tasks. And so, in March, 1981, four years after his initial referral to Clearview, Michael began to be mainstreamed into a regular classroom at Evers for part of the day, in order to see whether or not he could be in such a classroom on a full-time basis. It was difficult for him to be weaned from the behavior modification system Mrs. Sheppard had set up that year. Going to another class for part of the day meant not accumulating enough points for money or food reinforcers. It took several months for Michael to sense that the intrinsic rewards of being in a normal classroom were greater than the material reinforcers Mrs. Sheppard provided.

Greg Parnell, the teacher of the regular third grade class at Evers that Michael attended, was bewildered after meeting Michael. "Why," he asked, "was this boy called severely emotionally disturbed? How did he get sent to Clearview?" He saw Michael's problems as the same as those of other students in his class. Michael did get into a few fist-fights, but Greg saw this as "normal" behavior for boys. He felt that it was particularly normal for a child who was not clearly "in" with the group. Although this behavior was understood in the context of the child's world, Mr. Parnell made it clear to his students that he would not accept fighting or other disruptive behavior in the classroom. Like other teachers at Evers, he believed that clearly set rules and a clear understanding by the child of the consequences for rule violation are what is needed to manage a classroom. Greg Parnell also recognized the overriding importance of the child's family:

> I know that Michael is a hot-head. They did tell me that, and that he could pop right off. You see a lot of things that they put up with in those special education classes that I don't take here. They take things there because they want to take 'em, but I won't put up with it in here. And Michael can take what I give him. Like he loses his temper and starts yelling and screaming. That's out. I had that problem only one time and I sat with him and his mother about it. She says she don't got that problem with him and that if I discipline him, he won't do it. She felt that he wouldn't do it here and gave me a free hand to deal with him. And I think he knows I would if it ever came down to it.

As long as Michael remained at Evers, he would not be perceived as a child who is "really" emotionally disturbed. His behavior would be held in check by strict behavior management and/or the threat of corporal punishment. Teachers would, for the most part, be responsive to his emotional needs and consider his behavior within the context of his family and his neighborhood. Unfortunately, he also would not be challenged to stretch his intellectual and creative skills, nor would he be prepared for functioning in a world that expects individuals to know the rules, without always being given the rule book.

Carl Smith

Carl Smith entered Betty Olds' class in the Education Center in December 1978, when it was located in the old wing of the Evers School. He had been attending the Jones School, a kindergarten through sixth grade elementary school located in a predominantly middle class White neighborhood. Because of the growth of the Black population in the city, the redistricting of schools, and the Alternative Attendance program, Jones' Black population had grown from eight percent in 1965 to 27.8 percent in 1975, the year that Carl first entered kindergarten there. Many Black parents were attracted to Jones because of its reputation as a liberal school, the high academic achievement of its students, and its close proximity to the neighborhood where most Blacks lived.

The "Social History" outlined in Carl's records shows that he is the youngest of four children, the second-born of twins. Smaller at birth than his twin sister, Carl remained smaller and lagged behind her developmentally in social, emotional, and intellectual skills. The following description of Carl's family is taken from this "Social History":

> Carl's parents separated soon after the twins' birth. Mr. Smith still sees the children. He has cerebral palsy. One arm was afflicted and was amputated for the purpose of giving him a working claw. According to his family, a change in personality followed the amputation. Mrs. Smith found him difficult in his handling of the children, especially their older son, who was withdrawn and considered "retarded." This child is placed in an EMR [Educable Mentally Retarded] class.

> Carl also spends time with his paternal grandparents. His paternal grandfather and uncle are ministers. Because Mrs. Smith is working and has worked steadily, Carl and his twin sister have been in day care. Mrs. Smith has worked hard to provide well for her children. They are well-clothed and well-fed. The home, although in the housing projects, is attractively furnished, clean and neat. Mrs. Smith takes an interest in her children's education and visits the schools. She knows her children well, recognizes their problems and is always willing for [sic] help in working on them. There is a stepfather in the home, to whom the children adjust well.

> Mrs. Smith describes Carl as very generous, so much so that sometimes he forgets to include himself in his sharing. He has always been a friendly little boy and seems to know how to manipulate others. In the neighborhood, Carl

is very active in play out of doors. He generally gets along well with other children and does not fight.

Carl entered the Jones School in September 1975, as did his twin sister, as Alternate Attendance students. Both children attended a day-care center in the morning and the kindergarten program in the afternoon. Carl's attendance in kindergarten was short-lived. He would fall asleep frequently. His overall physical, cognitive, and social development were seen as somewhat delayed and he was returned to the day-care center on a full-time basis, while his sister continued to attend the Jones School's half-day kindergarten program. Carl returned to the Jones School's kindergarten the following September and is described in the school records as having "evidenced babyish behavior." An "Inventory of Readiness Skills" was administered at the end of his second kindergarten year, and Carl scored in the "high-average" range. He was promoted to first grade in the Fall of 1977.

Some question remained in the minds of the school personnel as to whether or not Carl should be in first grade fulltime, or in the kindergarten for half a day and attend first grade halftime. The building's Committee on the Handicapped discussed Carl's case and recommended that he be given a psychological evaluation and be seen by Dr. Flagg. Afterward, the committee recommended the following:

> ... because of his age and his tendency towards babyish behavior and to avoid academic tasks, we felt that he should be full-time first grade. Dr. Flagg saw Carl and noted his manipulative behavior and avoidance of academic tasks. It was Dr. Flagg's opinion that we leave Carl in the regular first grade class and insist that he produce the academic work.

Dr. Flagg's recommendations did not include a recognition of the possibility that Carl's behavioral problems were related to a difficulty with academic tasks. As a result, Carl remained in the first grade fulltime, and was placed in a *Distar* reading program. At the Jones School, *Distar* is perceived to be the appropriate program for children who are having difficulty in learning to read, particularly if they are Black children from low socioeconomic backgrounds.

An examination of Carl's records indicates that he may have been experiencing learning problems that required an approach not taken by the *Distar* method. In addition, the information provided in his social history should have alerted the school personnel that this was a child who could be perceived to be at risk for learning problems because of his low birth weight and early developmental delays. The fact that his twin sister was very successful in school should also have indicated that Carl's home environment could not be held as totally responsible for his academic failure.

Carl did not do well in *Distar* or with the classroom routine in general. In particular, Carl had difficulty in following directions and retaining information; as this evaluation points out:

> Transition from one activity to another is difficult. Arrivals and departures difficult, slow in moving, dawdles. Difficulty with following directions, needs them repeated several times and then often does not follow exactly. Structured routine is helpful. Seems to be motivated by audio-visuals and manipulative materials.
>
> Attitude: Sometimes defensive and also an "I can't do it" attitude.

His behavior is seen to have deteriorated over the course of that year, with him frequently throwing "temper tantrums." Teachers recall seeing Carl in the hallway, "continually" crying, sometimes screaming, and often behaving in ways they refer to as "babyish." His classroom teacher described him in the written records as being "very impulsive, often overly active and very dependent upon his teachers. He often disrupts the class by interrupting or bothering other children. His academic skills are poor and he seems to have difficulty paying attention and following directions."

The psychometric tests Carl received that year included a Wechsler Intelligence Scale for Children-Revised, on which he scored a Verbal I.Q. of 80, Performance I.Q. of 71, and Full Scale I.Q. of 74. These scores disqualified him from being identified as educable mentally retarded. However, his poor performance on the Bender-Gestalt, along with reported difficulties he was experiencing with auditory tasks and following directions, would have made a designation of learning disabled possible for this child. If this school had had a learning disabilities program at that time, Carl might have received appropriate services that could have helped keep him at the Jones School. Instead, Carl was reassigned to the first grade for the 1978–79 school year, so that he might continue to work in the *Distar* program, which he had failed the year before.

He was now eight years old. In his second year in first grade, Carl continued to behave in a disruptive manner and became even more distractible. Although he progressed in math, he was not able to retain the sounds of letters as required by the *Distar* program. The school's Committee on the Handicapped referred Carl once again to Dr. Flagg. The following comments were noted on district Committee on the Handicapped forms:

> Dr. Flagg evaluated Carl and again found him to be extremely manipulative. Instead of being babyish, Carl had become quite smug and spunky. He will

need SED [Severely Emotionally Disturbed]. His pediatrician has already recommended counseling. Dr. Flagg mentioned the Education Center.

In December 1978, Carl was transferred from the first grade at Jones School into Betty Olds' classroom in the Education Center, which was still in the old, back wing of Evers. I met Carl and his teachers in the Spring of 1980. At that time he was in his Education Center classroom for one hour a day, for the *Distar* language program, and in Mary Flynn's second-grade class for the rest of the day. Betty Olds had been his teacher for almost a year. This was her second year as a special education teacher and her second year in the Education Center. A young, always stylishly dressed White woman in her mid-twenties, Betty felt unprepared for the children she was faced with in her class. She had just completed a masters degree at Lakeside University in special education, with a focus on emotionally disturbed children. She felt she had learned a lot about behavior management and child counseling, but had never had the opportunity to work directly with a group of children on her own before she came to Evers.

A lack of self-confidence in her ability to manage her classroom was evident. Arguments between the children, as well as between the children and teacher, were a regular part of the day. Her behavior modification system was applied inconsistently. Academic work was often put on the back burner while Betty and her aide broke up a fight or tried to smoothe out a disagreement. She was not happy with the way her classroom was operating and was particularly upset about how difficult it was to get a child mainstreamed and eventually out of her room altogether. The biggest barrier to getting a child out was usually his low academic performance. In her classroom, she believed, a child who was academically behind might fall even further behind because of the lack of focus there on academics.

Question: So, do you think then, in your case, that the academic level of your kids would get in the way of their being mainstreamed?

Betty: Without a doubt. I have a nine year old—he'll be ten in July—and he's not reading on a second grade level yet.

Question: So one criterion, then, for a kid to "go out" is that he be somewhat close to the academic level of the corresponding class. How do you feel about that?

Betty: I feel that, well, I don't want to cop out on the answer, but I see that there are major difficulties with that. There is a big element of "Catch 22" with that. They are sent to us for behavioral clean-up, and if we do our jobs right and everything works out and we clean up their behavior, they have lost a year in the process. Of, if they came in a year behind, we keep them a year behind, and there is a big problem with that.

Question: So you don't get into too much academically, then? Is that what you're saying?

Betty: We get to do a good deal of academics, but you can't do everything in a vacuum. We try to change the behavior through the academics, but there has never been a week where I haven't lost at least one instruction group because of behavior. There is no way I could run my groups the way Mary Flynn runs her second grade.

Carl, like the other children in this classroom, had been designated as severely emotionally disturbed. To Betty Olds and the other teachers in the Education Center, this label signified that their primary responsibility was to work at modifying the child's social behavior. Academic performance came second. During one of my interviews with Betty, we reviewed Carl's records together. She was surprised to find out about the learning problems that had been diagnosed earlier:

I didn't know he was so low. . . . [Observer's Comment: she is referring to his tested I.Q.] Well, he was behind when he came to me, but he wasn't behind the kids in here. So whatever academic frustrations may or may not have existed, they disappeared when he walked in here.

Carl had failed in Distar at Jones School. When he was placed at Evers, the recommendation had been made that another reading program be used. However, since Evers and the Education Center were both "total Distar," Betty felt that there were no other options open, in spite of the fact that each child's educational program was supposed to be designed on an individual basis. Although the Individual Education Plan written for each child in the Education Center was written in behavioral language, stating each child's current level of functioning, long-term goals and short-term objectives, in reality these were no more individualized than was the program of any child at Evers. An assumption had been made about these children, based on the definition given to their overt behavior, and this assumption went on to influence their total educational program.

Fortunately, Distar was not the disaster Betty had anticipated. Instead, probably because Carl had been exposed to the same materials for two previous years, he became the highest reader in her class. Betty related an improvement in Carl's self-esteem to his success in academics in her classroom. However, since her focus for all her students was on "behavioral clean-up," it was the rapid change in his overt behavior that convinced her, after he had been in her classroom for only one month, that Carl was ready for "mainstreaming."

From the beginning of his placement in her classroom, Betty saw Carl as a child who responded well to a clearly defined set of expectations:

I don't think his ability to stay on one track and really analyze something is really top-notch or anything. . . . I feel that his behavior straightened out within a month. I think that other people mellowed out and I think that classroom expectations became clear. This is the work we do and this is the work you're expected to do. This will not be tolerated.

Betty's biggest problem became convincing other staff, particularly Laurie, the social worker, that Carl really did not need to be in her class any longer. According to Betty, Laurie "jumped on him" when he first arrived, not giving him adequate time to adjust.

Betty: When he came there were problems I would identify as adjusting to a new place. "Who knows what people are expecting of me?" problems. These problems were related in part to other adults in the building. I hesitate to talk about this because it does relate to other staff in the building. [*Observer's Comment*: At this point, I reassure Betty that her remarks are taken in confidence, that the identification of people will be disguised, and that my purpose here is to learn about the complexities involved in the operation of the program.] Well, my aide last year and I knew that Laurie did not like him when he first came here. There was a lot of difficulty with that. We went on a couple of field trips and she had a great deal of difficulty dealing with him, and I immediately felt that I had to jump in as an advocate for the kid.

Question: What was she doing?

Betty: Badgering him. It was like when we went to see Santa Claus. He had just arrived in the program that December. He said, "I don't want to see Santa Claus. I don't believe in Santa Claus." [*Observer's Comment*: I learned later that Carl's family were Jehovah's Witnesses, who did not celebrate Christmas.] So, she made him cry and go stand in the corner and said to him, "Don't you cry and don't you call me names." It was like she was backing him into the corner-type thing. It was difficult. Neither of us knew him well enough to know if that should be said to him. I hesitate to say it because everybody's been in a situation where they've done something wrong. But, in the case of Carl, I think that was part of why his adjustment was difficult for that first month.

The problems that existed between Carl and Laurie would continue to influence his program, particularly when the time came to return him to his original school. Although Laurie was opposed to his being mainstreamed at Evers, the consensus of other staff, both in the Education Center and in the school building as a whole was that Carl should be mainstreamed as quickly as possible. Carl's positive behavior in the cafeteria and other unstructured situations seemed to indicate he was ready. In addition, he was the highest reader in the special education class. In June 1979, Betty recommended that Carl be mainstreamed at Evers in September.

In November 1979, Carl entered Mary Flynn's regular second-grade class for math group, and accompanied her students to gym class each Thursday, following math. Each week, for six weeks, his time was increased until he was in Mary's room full-time, with the exception of one hour a day with Betty for *Distar* language, and any other support he might need. After two additional months of full-time placement in Mary's room, Carl was to be considered for return to the Jones School.

During these three and a half months in the second grade, Carl exhibited some of the same behaviors that had been described in his records as having occurred at the Jones School. Mary did not see this as an indication that Carl was, in fact, emotionally disturbed, but rather that he was using behaviors that he had learned in other settings. Some of these behaviors were seen as having come about because of his time in the Education Center. As Mary put it:

> It was very hard getting him to sit and do any independent work for a long time, coming from the Education Center, where there are two teachers, or a teacher and an aide and ten kids. Having to wait was a problem. If he's got a problem, somebody's picking on him, and I'm busy with something else, he just has to wait. That took a long time.

Other behaviors were seen as those he had learned in other situations as methods of getting out of an unpleasant situation:

> Well, just this morning he was brought in to me just after the bell rang, by another teacher. He had just been in an horrendous fight and totally lost control of his temper. One teacher tried to stop him and he just yanked away. I don't know if he cursed the teacher, and ran to the next room. The next teacher grabbed him with his shaking, the whole thing. I think that he's learned that if he plays he's out of control, people will kind of cater to him. Because, when he got him up here, I just said to him to stop and he could turn it right off. He's not out of control. He's no perfect angel, but he knows that I'm not going to take it.

Mary Flynn relates her ability to work effectively with Carl and with other students who have been described as "out of control" to her "expectations:"

> I think it's a matter of expectations. I expect Carl to act like the rest of them, absolutely. And I think what happens a lot of times is that people look at him and say, "Oh, he's crazy." They expect him to act in that way and allow for it. And so, of course, he does it. Kids do just about what you expect of them.

Mary recognized that her expectations might be different from what Carl would find when he returned to his home school. In addition, she was aware that although he fit in academically with the lowest reading group in her class, this group was far below the level expected in a regular second grade class in Jones School, which was known for its students' high achievement levels. However, she and the Evers Committee on the Handicapped felt that it was their responsibility to indicate that this child was not severely emotionally disturbed and to make the recommendation that he return to the school that had referred him.

Mrs. Smith, Carl's mother, had reportedly been involved in the decisions regarding Carl's program. It is not clear, however, what she or other parents of the boys in the Education Center had been told regarding the label given to their children, or the reason given for their placement. The form letter sent home from the district's special education office to the parents of these students indicated only that a child was being placed in a special education program "because of emotional reasons." Mrs. Smith may also have been told, informally, by Carl's teachers and/or the social worker that he was being placed in "a small class where your son will get the extra help he needs." Like most mothers of Education Center children, Mrs. Smith was grateful for the help she believed was being offered.

Everyone at Evers had expected that Mrs. Smith would agree to have Carl returned to the Jones School at the end of his three-month mainstreaming program at Evers. However, when the time came, to most everyone's surprise, she refused to give her permission. She stated that she wanted him to continue at Evers because he was getting the help he needed and that he was not "in trouble" there, as he had been at Jones. No one at Evers could offer an explanation for her change of mind, but Betty Olds indicated her feeling that Laurie's communications with this mother may have played a part in this turn of events:

> I told his mother that his skills were good, that his behavior was tremendous, and that I wanted to send him back to Jones School. I felt that she thought it was great, as soon as he's ready to go. That's in a nutshell what I thought was happening. I talked with her every two or three weeks. Letting her know that he was continuing to progress. Near the end, when we needed the building committee forms signed by her, Laurie took them out to her to sign and she said that she wanted him to stay until June.

As a result, Carl stayed at Evers until June, and returned to Jones in September 1980. He was relabeled from severely emotionally disturbed to emotionally disturbed, and placed in a regular third grade classroom, with one hour a day to be spent in a Resource Room. A careful match was made with a teacher that the Jones School's Committee on the Handicapped felt "could best meet his needs." Each classroom at Jones is now considered by its administration for the placement of any child in terms of its numbers of children by race, sex, and handicapping condition, to assure balanced classrooms throughout the building. Carl's classroom is about 50 percent

White and has a slightly larger percentage of girls than boys. There are three other children designated as handicapped in this room.

Jane Marney, the teacher of this class, is a young Black woman who spent most of her childhood in Lakeside. My observations of her classroom, her perspectives on her role as a teacher, and the methods she employs in her classroom were consistent with those things reported in the literature and by others in this study as the ingredients necessary for successful programming for students with behavioral and academic difficulties. In particular, she demonstrated that her students are given a clear idea of her expectations regarding their academic performance and behavior. Directions are carefully explained, both orally and in writing.

Her expectations for individual children are based upon what she comes to know about each child after he or she is in her classroom for a while. However, the entire class is expected to conform to some basic principles of behavior that are clearly spelled out. The consequences for rule breaking are also clear. Jane describes her approach as focused on "prevention":

> What I try to do here is to prevent problems. You know, create the kind of atmosphere where the kids know exactly how to deal with things. Of course, a lot depends on the kid and for each problem or each thing that happens you really have to find out why the behavior occurred. You know, on the first day of school I let kids know what I expect of them and what they can expect of me. So it's very clear.

Although Jane describes herself as "highly structured," her classroom does not appear to be operating within the same tight regimen as did Evers classrooms. There is an appearance of casualness in her room, with students talking to each other quietly during work times and frequently getting out of their seats. However, not too far beneath the surface is an organized classroom, well controlled by this teacher. I observed a clearly articulated routine and students' behavior adapting appropriately to each different activity. Jane helped some students through transitions by preparing them for what was to happen next and by clarifying what would be expected of them. This was done both by her announcing the coming activity and by having written the day's schedule on the chalkboard.

By looking at each student's behavior within the context of each individual's needs, Jane operates an almost individually structured program. She has divided the class of 26 students into six reading groups and allows the more advanced students to help each other with their individual assignments, while she spends more time with the slower students. At the same time, group enrichment activities are often presented to the class as a whole by the more advanced students, individually or through group projects. The room is decorated with many of these projects and, unlike the classrooms at Evers, there are a many books and materials available for use by the children during their free time.

Jane believes that it is important to foster children's independent thinking skills. She feels that highly regimented programs like *Distar*, although providing the essential skills needed for reading, limit children's learning:

> *Distar* is ridiculous. You can't teach it in a large class. There's no way you can follow exactly what *Distar* says and keep kids step by step the way it's laid out.
>
> I think that any kid who is both in *Distar* and special ed. has a double handicap. They have been kept back because they have to move at the pace of the *Distar* group, plus in special ed., they miss the opportunities to learn what kids in a regular class get.

Jane has never seen behavior from Carl that would indicate to her that he needed a special education placement. She is not aware of what he had done previously, but feels that he is now a child who can control his behavior and has developed many coping devices. She feels that even if he was misbehaving in an immature or irresponsible manner, it was the regular classroom teacher's responsibility to deal with his behavior. She elaborates:

> The idea of labeling a kid just because he is childish, irresponsible and immature is absolutely terrible. What happens in special ed. is that the kids are allowed to slide so much that they miss out.

Carl's behavior toward me was remarkably different in this environment than it had been in either the Education Center or in Mary Flynn's classroom. At Evers, Carl became concerned by my continual presence in his classroom. He was certain that I was there to evaluate him, and was reluctant to talk with me. "Whenever I see people who are all around," as he put it, "I'm sure they're watching me." However, when I came to observe Jane Marney's room, Carl seemed quite pleased and asked his teacher if he could introduce me to the class. Carl stood next to me at the back of the room and announced, "This is my friend Judy. She is from my other school, Medgar Evers, from the Education Center. She can help you with whatever you want, so come right back here and ask her if you need any help."

Carl was also able to share his perspective with me regarding his placement at Evers and his return to Jones.

Carl: Well, you know I used to be in the Education Center. First I was in this school and they sent me to the Education Center. And then they sent me back here because I was doing real good.

"Severely Emotionally Disturbed"

Question: Why were you sent to the Education Center?

Carl: Well, they said I needed a smaller class. And then I was real good in my small class and they sent me to Miss Flynn's room.

Question: Which place did you like better?

Carl: At the Evers School kids mess around too much and you have to defend yourself and sometimes I did and I had to fight there. In the Education Center there were lots of fights and kids get you in trouble. They're always starting off. I really didn't like the paddling they did. The principal was real mean. [*Observer's Comment*: I later discovered he is referring to Laurie, as she was the only person who ever spoke of paddling Carl.] She'd take me into the office and then know what she'd make you do? She'd make you bend over this chair [He demonstrates, pushing the chair out in front of him, putting his hands on the chair while bending forward], tie your hands down on the chair and paddle you real hard. I didn't like that, especially all the messing around and paddling. But my teacher, she was real good and we had all kinds of good things there. We would go to Pizza Hut and she'd take us to her house. She got married and moved away. Her name was Miss Olds. Do you know her?

Carl has adjusted well to his return to Jones, according to both Jane Marney and his resource teacher, Barry Parker. Barry sees his role as one of aiding in this adjustment by providing reinforcement for academic skills and emotional support. Carl's one hour at the end of the day in the Resource Room often focuses on an "affective education" program. For example, Carl may read stories about children who are experiencing problems and answer questions related to his feelings about what went on in the stories. Barry explains the importance of Carl's time in the Rersource Room:

> This gives Carl the opportunity to verbalize his feelings and to think out and plan in logical sequences something that is difficult for him.

Above the chalkboard in the Resource Room, children's pencil and crayon drawings were on display. Several of these were done by Carl. Figure 7.1 is a "reproduction" of one of Carl's drawings, done during the first weeks of his return to the Jones School. It shows this child's attempts to clarify the "rules" to himself and adjust to this new environment.

At this school, as at other middle-class schools, children were expected to know the rules that define appropriate behavior. At Evers, these were spelled out to students by every classroom teacher and reinforced by strict sanctions for misbehavior. Carl had learned that if he wanted to stay out of trouble, which to him now meant returning to the Education Center, he had better remember the rules and obey them, even if other kids did not. He had also learned that one way he could remember things clearly was to

FIGURE 7.1
Carl's View of His New School's "Rules"

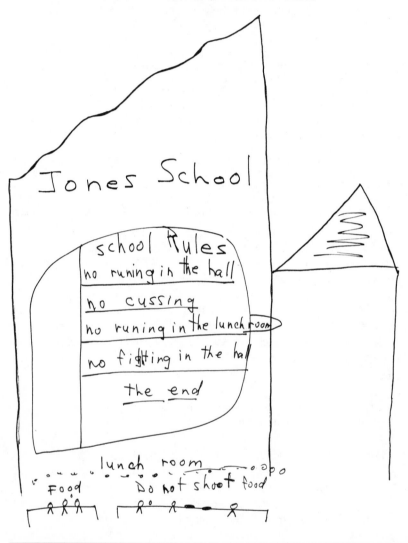

write them out, when he could. Carl would succeed because he had learned how to teach himself the rules.

The popular perception of the Jones School in Lakeside is that it is one of the best elementary schools in the city. Not only was it considered to be outstanding in academic achievement, as evidenced by the highest standardized reading scores in the city, but the social behavior of its students was also considered to be exemplary. Contrary to popular perceptions, the behavior of its students, as observed in hallways, the cafeteria, and its playground was more like what I had expected to find at Evers, but rarely saw there. The noise level in the Jones cafeteria was deafening, children were continually out of their seats, and teachers could often be seen reprimanding students. Snow ball fights and other minor altercations were common on the playground, as were "boys verses girls" battles. Children did not walk in quiet, orderly lines, as they did at Evers. At Jones, movement through the halls was noisy and playful.

Carl's earlier inability to cope with the environment at Jones was not seen as a "mismatch" between a child who needed a structured, highly predictable environment and a relatively "loose" school. Because Jones was not perceived in this way, and because some aspects of Carl's background (poor, Black, male child, living with a single mother) fit into the model under which Dr. Flagg operated, this child's problems were perceived to be the result of an emotional disturbance. The consequences of this were that Carl's intellectual needs were ignored to the point where he fell further and further behind in his academic skills. Jane Marney sees the lack of focus on the academic skills of poor, Black children in general as the result of the lowered expectations held for these children's ability to learn:

> It gets me really angry that teachers have certain assumptions when they see Black kids. They just assume automatically that they are not as bright as White kids. Not only do they assume that, but they also have expectations about who these kids are going to be, and where they are going to go. I don't want my child to go to the schools here and deal with the racism I had to face when I went to school in Lakeside. I grew up here and I was one of the only Black kids in the school at the time. A lot of the stuff that went on was subtle, but there were things that happened to me that I will never forget. I remember one thing that strikes me. I was in the fourth grade and I was fooling around. I wasn't doing my work. I was a wise guy, no question about it. But the thing the teacher said to me she never would have said if I was White. She turned to me and said in front of the whole class, "You're going to grow up to be a ditch-digger someday."

> It isn't just a Black-White thing. It's also the part of town you come from, for what they expect. If you grow up in the projects, right away, "What do you expect?" But if you have a kid who grows up in the Heights and he's a doctor's son, well, everybody expects him to do real well in school. When he does less well, the people really push him. When the poor kids from the projects don't do well, people say, "Well, what do you expect?"

And yet, both Jane and Carl were able to break out of a cycle often described as a "self-fulfilling prophecy" (Pidgeon, 1970; Rosenthal & Jacobson, 1968; Rubovits & Maehr, 1973). This does not necessarily invalidate the notion that this phenomenon operates, but, rather, illustrates that if individuals are given the opportunity to behave in ways that do not reinforce the meaning given to their behavior by others, the interaction cycle can be broken. This is, however, very difficult in the case of individuals who have become identified as "mentally ill." In spite of the fact that most of the Evers staff agreed during Carl's first few months there that the label of severely emotionally disturbed was inappropriate, it took two full years for Carl to shed that label.

The behaviors of the "disturbed" person often become redefined as illustrations of his or her disturbance (Rosenhan, 1973). Investigations have shown that teachers hold strong stereotypes regarding the meaning of "emotional disturbance" that bias their expectations and evaluations of labeled children (Foster, Ysseldyke & Reese, 1975; Salvia & Meisels, 1980; Vacc & Keist, 1977; Ysseldyke & Foster, 1978). Salvia and Meisels (1980) found, for example, that "observers tend to see or interpret behavior in a manner congruent with their stereotypes of the exceptionality. Thus, a child labeled 'emotionally disturbed' may be viewed as more aggressive than the same child labeled 'mentally retarded'" (p. 270).

Carl was placed in a situation at Evers where many people fortunately had become sensitive to the fact that minority children were often inappropriately labeled. His lack of aggressive behavior after one month in the Education Center was taken as an indication that he should not be in that program. This decision was not based on his teacher's belief that the other boys were "really disturbed," while Carl was not, but rather, her concern was that he might develop the negative behaviors to which he would be exposed. Betty Olds put it this way: "He was doing nothing here except being exposed to bizarre behavior. There was no way that this was the right setting for him."

The question to be asked, then, is if programs such as the Education Center are the right setting for *any* child. Placing behavior disordered children together in one classroom creates an environment in which the children feed off each other's weaknesses. Teachers' strategies seem to range from keeping tight external controls over children's behavior to those approaches that focus on the development of strong, positive relationships. In either case children's academic skills are ignored. None of these strategies presents a realistic picture of a more normalized school environment. Unfortunately, the school's inability to understand and program for children with different behavioral and learning characteristics is what was responsible for the development of these kinds of segregated programs in the first place.

8

Conclusion

Evers and the Emotionally Disturbed Child

Programs, policies, and practices evolve in school systems in response to more than the needs of the children they serve. In Lakeside, political pressures, such as the mandate to integrate schools, provide services to handicapped children, and improve the academic standing of low-income, minority children, combined with teachers' growing concern over maintaining control in their classrooms. This concern was not entirely unfounded. In Lakeside, as in many other northeastern cities, classrooms in ghetto schools during the 1960s were not places where children learned either the academic or social skills they needed. Teachers were confused and angry. Approaches that "worked" with middle-class White children failed to keep "these kids" in their seats and doing their work. Something needed to be done.

From the late 1960s through the end of the 1970s, regular and special education programs were developed to deal with this problem. Unfortunately, in Lakeside the programs were established with little input from the families of those children for whom they were intended. Certainly, soliciting the opinions of parents who may be alienated from formal schooling would not have been easy. These parents may not have known what educational options would be best for their child. However, they did know their own children and their habits, needs, interests, and skills. The PEEL Program might have included "enrichment" activities that expanded these abilities. Instead "enrichment" meant the teaching of foreign languages, classical music, and literature presented at reading levels above those of many Evers' children. Their interests and skills were not valued.

Direct input from parents into the content and form of an educational program not only promotes a better fit between the child's life in school and out but also heightens families commitment toward "their" school. In the process of becoming involved in educational decision making, parents learn the system. This knowledge will be invaluable throughout their child's school life. My personal experiences with several Head Start pro-

137

grams where low-income parents were true decision makers, have demonstrated the feasibility of parental involvement in program and policy decisions. Parental investment in their child's education increased when they were a part of program planning. These parents were also able to educate teachers about their children's lives outside of school. In Lakeside, the long history of de facto segregation had limited contacts between Blacks and Whites. Teachers and school officials therefore based their understanding of low-income Black children and their families on the interactions that occurred in school, defined from an ethnocentric perspective. This understanding was further reinforced by much of the literature on "culturally deprived" children written during the 1960s and early 1970s (Baratz & Baratz, 1973; Henry, 1971; Riessman, 1962; Valentine, 1968).

The official understanding of the causes of the problems faced by Black children in Lakeside clearly represent this perspective. Assumptions are made about individual children and their families based on stereotypes. Like all stereotypic thinking, these assumptions have some basis in reality. Certainly the young, single mother, living in the housing projects, supported by Aid to Families with Dependent Children, is in an often desperate situation. The children raised in these families do not live an idealized childhood, free from the anxieties of the material struggle faced by their mothers. Many of these children are troubled. However, in spite of obstacles, many manage not only to survive but to develop into bright, happy, and inquisitive children. Their mothers are rarely given public affirmation. At Evers, successful, well-functioning children are invisible to most of their teachers.

The instructional approach used at Evers today is based on the belief that all its students have similar needs. The majority of Evers' staff believe that the failure of programs in the past that attempted to provide diversity and enrichment for students proved that "these kids" could not benefit from enrichment programs. What is not recognized, however, is that these programs failed because they were developed—not with any real understanding of students' needs—but rather as remedies for the complex problems facing the school system. The PEEL Program, for example, was developed as a means of altering the negative image that Evers presented both to the citizens of Lakeside and to federal and state monitors. It was, after all, an all-Black school with an atrocious academic record.

It was not even considered that the placing of hundreds of high-achieving middle class and upper middle class children at Evers could have a negative effect on the neighborhood children. The failure of the indigenous Evers child to keep up with the imported child's academic pace only confirmed teachers' beliefs in the inferiority of their students. The new students functioned well in an open, enriched program, while the regular

Evers students needed clearly defined rules and lacked basic skills. Rather than recognizing that this predicament indicated a need to teach their children how to think independently, problem solve and be creative, it reinforced the notion that the neighborhood children were failures because they were unsocialized, unloved, and lacking in the basic intellectual skills necessary for independent thinking.

Although Black parents agreed that the PEEL Program failed to meet the needs of their children, their understanding of this failure is significantly different from that of school officials. From their perspective, it was the school that failed, not their children. The school was not meeting their children's academic needs, nor did it take into account the fact that the open environment, which was a part of this program, conflicted with the strict discipline their children received at home. Today, Evers' parents and teachers agree that this program and others that followed in the early 1970s ignored students' academic needs and followed an approach that did not match their home experiences. This understanding is the basis on which *Distar* was adopted as the school's total educational program.

The *Distar* programs symbolize an approach that characterizes a broad and popular trend in American education. On the surface, it appears as though these programs are at last providing for the academic and social needs of low-income, minority students by combining the latest in instructional technology with an appreciation for the culture of its students. The children at Evers are well behaved and are learning the "basics." However, Evers is still behind every other elementary school in Lakeside in both reading and mathematics achievement. Evers' students move into the Jefferson Middle School in the fifth grade. Teachers there report that although they are the best behaved of any group of incoming students, the average Evers student has a good deal of difficulty with fifth-grade academic material and is dependent on his or her teacher for problem solving. The independent thinking and abstract conceptualizations necessary for mastery of upper grade-level skills have not been developed in most of these children.

In tracing the development of American public schools, Katz (1971) demonstrated how northeastern industrial cities such as Lakeside have historically used educational practices that would teach conformity and obedience to working- and lower-class children. In the following statement, he describes the form of pedagogy prescribed by DeWitt Clinton in 1809 for the education of lower-class children. Its methods and goals are reminiscent of those of *Distar*:

> Aside from its miniscule cost per pupil, this mechanistic form of pedagogy, which reduced education to drill, seemed appropriate because the schools

served lower-class children who could without offense be likened to un-
finished products, needing to be inculcated with norms of docility, clean-
liness, sobriety and obedience. (p. 10)

The adoption of *Distar* as Evers' total academic program and the strict
behavioral management of its students have resulted in a school that appears to have responded to its students in a "new" way. In fact, what has
happened at Evers represents what educational reforms have meant historically in most of America's public schools: methods have changed, while
the basic assumptions of the schools have remained the same. The failure of
more radical changes in the 1960s and 1970s—such as those proposed by
Mr. Carp, incorporating participatory decision making, the child's understanding of his or her own behavior, active learning, and a recognition of
the value of affective and artistic education—can therefore, be understood
by their lack of fit with the priorities set by the school system.

The Evers teacher has learned through his or her experiences with the
children and families in this neighborhood and from the literature on the
education of "deprived" children what will "work," i.e., what will control
their behavior so that they may be the passive recipients of the information
he or she presents. Certainly, it is important that the children at Evers learn
basic reading and language skills. The *Distar* approach has proven itself to
be successful in teaching decoding skills and linear approaches to language.
However, by its being the *only* approach used at Evers, no opportunities are
provided for students to develop the creative processes and independent
thinking skills that will be needed for their economic survival and for the
enhancement of the quality of their lives, to say nothing of their academic
success beyond the early elementary school years.

Evers has been able to achieve something, however, that many of the
other schools in Lakeside have not. An understanding of its students' social
behavior has developed, which is qualitatively different from that of other
Lakeside schools. At Evers, the angry or disobedient child is not perceived
as deviant, but is instead viewed as a child who is responding to the circumstances in his or her life or as modeling behaviors seen in the community.
Teachers are not afraid of their students' aggressive behavior and feel prepared to deal with it within the contexts of their classrooms.

For the students who became labeled as severely emotionally disturbed
at other schools and were later sent to Evers, their previous school experiences were somewhat different. Their teachers also expected students to
conform to the rules of appropriate behavior. However, these teachers expected that their students knew, for the most part, what these rules were
and what behaviors were considered appropriate. For some children, the
teacher's lack of specific or consistent instructions meant that they could

do what they wanted. For others, their teachers' being intimidated by street language, an angry outburst, or a swagger meant they could avoid difficult academic tasks or bully their way into being first or getting the best toy. This behavior may have then been reinforced by the White, female teacher's preconceived fears of Black males and stereotypical images of "mental illness." By this point, the child's behavior was probably beyond what the teacher could manage. The next step would be a referral to the psychologist, then to the Committee on the Handicapped, and finally to Dr. Flagg.

Dr. Flagg is hopefully not representative of the psychiatric profession. Yet, he is real, and the quoted statements attributed to him are accurate. Others like him in other cities, perhaps in other positions, wield similar power and influence. As a doctor, he legitimizes the segregation of children under the guise of science. His distortions of the psychoanalytic perspective have led the Lakeside school district into developing programs based on "blaming the victim" rather than exploring the interactions that occur between children, families and schools. He cannot, however, be seen simply as an isolated example of a single, aberrant individual. His point of view serves an important function for the school system he represents.

By labeling disruptive students as severely emotionally disturbed, Dr. Flagg has allowed the Lakeside school system to circumscribe its responsibility for these students' education. No one interviewed for this study, other than Dr. Flagg and the pupil services director, believed the severely emotionally disturbed label to be an accurate diagnosis. However, designating these students as disturbed provided the system with an administrative device for removing difficult to manage Black children from predominantly White schools during a time when the school district was under pressure from federal and state governments to integrate its schools. Placing a troublesome student in a special education classroom gave the appearance of serving the child's best interests. There is nothing that indicates that the education received in the Education Center classrooms was more appropriate than that which the children had received in the classrooms from which they had been removed. In fact, as this study has illustrated, many of the students fell behind in their academic skills.

Enriching a child's cognitive development may not be given a high priority if his or her behavior is viewed as presenting a danger to other students and teachers. This would be understandable. Although the majority of young childeren in special education programs for the emotionally disturbed present no real physical danger, their behavior has frightened their teachers. This fear may have kept some regular classroom teachers from confronting the very behaviors they wished to change. Although the Education Center teachers were willing to confront disruptive behavior directly, they had less success at changing students' behavior than did the teachers in the regular classrooms at Evers. In the Education Center, disruptive behavior was reinforced both by the interactions that occurred between students and the lack of appropriate peer models in their classroom.

Gajar (1977), Hallahan and Kauffman (1977), and Quay and Galvin (1970) point out that although most children identified as emotionally disturbed display deficits in academic achievement, many special education programs for these children do not attend to their academic needs. This represents the failure to recognize the interactive relationship between thoughts and feelings. For the child who is successful in school, cognitive and affective needs are being met and reinforce each other in a positive manner. Clearly, looking only at a child's social behavior as a means of identifying his needs is looking at only half the child (Long, Morse, & Newman, 1980).

The focus on modifying the social behavior of Black children is reinforced by the low expectations held for these children's academic performance. Standardized testing reinforces these expectations by the "empirical" evidence it supposedly provides. A borderline score on a standarized I.Q. test is often interpreted as an indication of a student's limited potential when it may, instead, be indicative of the child's limited experiences. Rather then providing such children with experiences that will enrich their cognitive development, they are taught by rote drill, with materials whose content does little to stimulate the imagination. The process of learning that involves the active exploration by the student is assumed to be beyond their reach. These children are therefore never provided with these kinds of experiences and so never develop into active and motivated learners or problem solvers. Instead, they become passive recipients of the information that their teachers have chosen for them.

P.L. 94-142 and the Overrepresented

P.L. 94–142 was designed to provide an appropriate education for all children, regardless of their handicapping condition. As this study has shown, this legislation provides a means of labeling children who are perceived as deviant, i.e., those children whose behavior and/or learning styles do not match a school system's concept of normalcy. In Lakeside, this has allowed schools to maintain educational practices that may not match the lifestyles or learning styles of some of its children by identifying these children as handicapped. This has resulted in the overrepresentation of Black children and males among those labeled as emotionally disturbed.

This study has demonstrated how the judgments of teachers and other school officials are, in part, responsible for such overrepresentation.

The consequences of the overrepresentation of Black male children as emotionally disturbed has been illustrated in the experiences of Michael Thomas and Carl Smith. That both boys managed to work their way out of the special education sytem might be seen as evidence that there are workable checks and balances within the system. However, this line of reasoning fails to recognize that a significant portion of these boys' educational careers were devoted to figuring out how to outsmart their teachers and survive with other students, instead of developing their academic abilities and positive social skills. These children have been robbed of important childhood years.

The U.S. General Accounting Office (1981) survey on the disparities in special education services throughout the United States validates what was found in Lakeside. On a national level, males are clearly overrepresented in all categories of handicapping conditions, and most severely overrepresented among those labeled emotionally disturbed. There are three times as many boys identified as emotionally disturbed as there are girls. Since the determination of emotional disturbance lies largely in the subjective judgment of teachers and other school officials, this disparity can be seen to be the result of those biases that relate to the perception of normal and appropriate behavior.

Aggressiveness is a quality that American culture values in males. However, boys often experience difficulty in school when behaviors (e.g., assertiveness, physical contact) that are reinforced in other environments conflict with expectations regarding appropriate behavior in schools. For Black boys, the situation is compounded by the position Black men have held, historically, in our society. The "acting out" behavior seen in some Black male children in public schools needs to be be understood within the context of the meaning their behavior has for their teachers and other school officials. The interactions that have occurred between these children and the significant adults in their lives become defined by these adults.

The concept of a "culture of poverty" that dominated the social science literature during the middle through late 1960s has been incorporated into these definitions. Much of this literature and that which came before it focused on the Black family as the purveyor of pathology (Kardiner, 1959; Moynihan, 1965). Dr. Flagg's position, for example, echoes the "tangle of pathology" described in the widely publicized "Moynihan Report". The following passage taken from this report was published in *Newsweek* in August 1965, before its official release:

> Negro woman are . . . forced to take jobs thus *undermining the man's role as the breadwinner* [emphasis added] . . . The father stays on as an ineffectual

dependent or he drifts off, perhaps to the few remaining places where a ravaged man can assert his manhood: in the bedroom or in the street. Either way the model he presents to his sons is one of futility, alienation, and despair. Family discipline breaks down and so does performance. (Ryan, 1971, p. 63)

The extensive media coverage of this document conveyed to the public as well as to professionals, a perspective that explained the problems of Blacks in terms of their pathology.

The Black family has been described in terms of White, middle-class definitions that do not include the social networks that are an integral part of the Black family. References to these support systems were heard frequently at Evers by both typical students and those from the Education Center. Children would often be cared for by "grands," "aunts," and "uncles." Many children would refer to each other as "cousins." Young men would often bring children to school or meet them at the end of the day. Although often not the child's biological father, these men were stable figures in the child's life, offering the male "role model" assumed to be absent from their lives.

Being a young, single, Black mother in the 1980s, trying to raise children on the limited support offered by Aid to Families with Dependent Children, is a stressful and often depressing way of life. Ethnocentric definitions of the family place the responsibility for the dilemma faced by these women and their children on the women themselves and ignore the economic and social forces acting upon them. Dr. Flagg allows no way out for the Black mother. Those women who are able to find employment are still perceived as inadequate. Dr. Flagg describes this thusly:

> Now you have all these Black mothers and what are they doing? They're out working. Working middle-class Black women. And they have decided that they don't need men anymore. They don't need men. They don't need marriage. And they have put all their problems off on Black men. Instead now they come home and they are tired after work and they don't want to be bothered by their daughters or their sons now. So they are off and independent. At least the mothers on AFDC are home. They give some nurturing to the kids even if they are rejecting. These mothers don't do anything.

In defining single mothers as pathological, Dr. Flagg has failed to recognize that the world being experienced by the Black child in the 1980s is in some ways quite different from that of the 1960s and early 1970s. Single-parent families are being redefined by the rest of society. Single mothers are not perceived as deviant as they were in the past. Hopefully, the single, Black mother will benefit by the larger society's growing awareness of the needs of single-parent families. In Lakeside this can be seen by the growing, but still inadequate numbers of day-care centers, publicly funded preschools, and full day kindergartens.

Jean Baker-Miller (1982) conducted a brief study of a group of eight low-income, single mothers who, although having suffered psychological distress and economic and social hardship, developed what they defined as positive lives for themselves and their children. Contrary to Dr. Flagg's perspective, these women demonstrated that the enhancement of their self-worth that developed through their work or return to school added to their relationships with their children. Dr. Miller, a psychoanalytically trained psychiatrist, feels that the picture portrayed in in the psychiatric literature of the necessarily negative effects of single parenthood on children may be the result of a selectivity factor. Most of the women in her study were in "terrible shape" during the early stages of their separation. This is the period of time when most were seen for psychiatric help. However, over time, these women were seen to develop strategies that not only helped them to cope, but that improved the quality of life for them and their children.

A further implication of Dr. Miller's work relates to the understanding of "misbehavior" by children who are living in stressful living situations. In some cases these stresses are transient and the child can be helped to ride-out the difficulties he is experiencing at home by the support he receives from other adults and peers. If, however, others react to his negative behavior with fear and/or rejection, as was the case for most of the children in the Education Center, the child's behavior may escalate and become reinforced. When a child who is in a transient state of "disturbance" as the result of the stresses in his or her life and/or the pressures he or she feels at school becomes identified as emotionally disturbed, this state becomes perceived as more or less permanent. There certainly are children whose lives can be characterized as a series of traumatic events, interrupted only by brief periods of respite. Black children, living in low income families that have been unable to offer the nurturing and security children need, are some of these children. But, there are many others.

In Lakeside, for example, Black families are rarely reported for child abuse. This may not mean that there are no abused Black children in Lakeside but rather suggests that there are many White children with emotional problems who have been neglected by the schools. In another Lakeside school I visited, teachers expressed their concern about two young White girls in their classes who had been sexually abused in their homes. Both girls were described as very withdrawn and fearful of any sort of contact with either children or adults. Their teachers were frustrated by the lack of supportive services for these girls. If a child was not "acting out" or significantly behind in academic work, then he or she could not be labeled as disturbed and therefore was not eligible for supportive services.

The overrepresentation of one segment of the population in any classification system implies that there may be another group that is underrepresented. Since the designation of emotional disturbance is often used as a way to provide programs for aggressive children (Grosenick & Huntze, 1980), severely withdrawn and fearful children may be neglected. Girls who behave in this way are often ignored in school, since they create no real management problems for their teachers and because it is assumed that passivity is normal and appropriate for females. Because a designation of severe emotional disturbance is used in Lakeside as a means of removing disruptive children from regular classrooms, there is no longer any real option within this school district for those children who may, for a short period of time, need a small, well-structured and highly supportive learning environment. One intent of Peter Stein's original program was to create such a setting.

Don Canby, Evers' school social worker, was familiar with the old Education Center and compared today's students with those of the past:

> I would say as a whole, you see a lot better behavior than you used to. It's not as bad as it used to be. We have one boy who really goes all the time and he really needs those kinds of classes (i.e., the old Education Center). Overall, I don't think the program gets as many, I don't want to use the word "bad" but, children with severe behavorial problems as they used to. One thing is that we have to deal with it in a school setting and that may be it too. We don't have anywhere to send them such as the old Education Center that was downtown. There are some we can't put any place because of their behavior. They can't go in the classroom. We have one here right now and there is no place for him because he doesn't fit in the classroom. Now that's where the old C.A.A. center would have met his needs.

The boy he is describing, Dayrell, had been in Dan Pallard's class for two years. In his first year, Dan's class was located in the older wing of the building. Dan felt that Dayrell could be managed in that setting. Although only ten years old, this child was quite large and would use his size to intimidate other students. His academic skills were poor, as was his ability to communicate verbally. Dayrell and his younger brother had been twice sent "down South" by their mother to avoid their removal from her home by the Department of Social Services. She is described as an excessive alcoholic. Unfortunately, neither Dayrell's grandparents nor the southern school he attended could cope with him. He was returned to Lakeside but his brother remained with the "grands."

When Dayrell returned to school in September 1980, he was again placed in Mr. Pallard's class, which was now in the main wing of Evers. He was unable to cope with the large numbers of children with whom he had to interact. He became violent, throwing chairs and attacking other students and teachers. His mother came to school drunk, threatening to beat him and anyone else who got in her way. Dayrell was removed from her custody, placed in a foster home, and given home-bound instruction until a decision could be made regarding a more appropriate placement.

There were no programs for Dayrell in the community. The Clearview School, a privately operated day treatment program and school for young children labeled as severely emotionally disturbed, saw him as too dangerous and needing a firmer hand than they imposed on their students. It was agreed that although this child had not yet committed a crime, he needed to be placed in a prison-like facility. Dayrell had learned that he could use his size to intimidate adults, keeping them at a distance. Six months later, he was placed in a maximum security, residential treatment center in another part of the state.

Dayrell's mother was blamed for his situation. This "blaming" somehow seemed to negate providing her with the help she needed to raise her two sons. Although it certainly would not have solved all of this family's problems, a program in the community, somewhat more restrictive than the Education Center had become, coupled with direct support for his mother might have allowed this child to remain in the community. This type of program could have worked together with the family to maximize the possibility of their reuniting. Unfortunately, a range of services for children with behavorial and family problems does not exist in Lakeside.

By using the label severely emotionally disturbed for children who present behavior problems to their teachers, Lakeside has altered its definition of this population. In doing so it has found a way to deal with large numbers of disturbing children in a cost effective manner that would not require any significant alterations in the school systems. As a result, children with disruptive behaviors have been stigmatized by an inappropriate label while other children who are in need of intervention have no programs available to them in their community. Since special education classes for the severely emotionally disturbed have been used by this school system as places to send disruptive boys from low-income families, school buildings' Committees on the Handicapped will rarely refer girls or the more affluent White students to Dr. Flagg for consideration of a label of emotional disturbance. They fear that these children will be "eaten alive" if placed in a typical S.E.D. class. They also know that a more affluent parent would object to such a placement once the composition of the class was made apparent.

The one White student in the Education Center that I came to know told me about his initial reaction to his special education class. Steve, like the other White boys here, was from a low-income family. He lived with his mother, who was an older woman, unemployed, and in poor health.

> Well, at first I was pretty scared. I had never known any Black kids before and I thought they were going to be really tough, beat me up and stuff. My mom

was scared too but they told her that it would help me. But they're not so bad. Don't fight no more than the kids in my other school and we have a real good time. They do use swear words more than White kids. That's about it.

In Lakeside, middle-class White students who display "inappropriate" behavior along with academic failure will more often be labeled as learning disabled. This happens both as a way to avoid the severely emotionally disturbed label and placement in a situation with low-income and minority students. Among middle class parents, the learning disability designation has become an acceptable label (Bogdan & Kugelmass, 1984). This identification now offers an explanation for their child's failure in school. He is no longer perceived as lazy or stupid or as a bad kid. Instead, he does not do well in school because he is "sick." He has a condition that is not his fault. He has a learning disability. This label removes the responsibility for the child's failure from the child, his family, and the school. It also allows everyone, including the child, to believe that beneath the school failure lies the possibility of success in the future. After all, a child with a learning disability has, by definition, average or above average potential.

Low-income Black children are, on the other hand, expected to do poorly on academic tasks. This, in part, explains their underrepresentation among those labeled as learning disabled. A child is identified as learning disabled when there is believed to be a discrepancy between academic performance and potential. This underachievement is believed to be the outcome of a disorder in the child's sensory processing skills, the integration of these skills, or in a learning style that does not match that which is demanded for success on the tasks presented in school. In either case, this type of disorder is based on what is believed to be a biological deficit within the child. It is not understood to be the result of environmental deprivation. Since Black children from low-income families are seen as children who are culturally deprived, and since it is often assumed that their potential is less than that of the average middle class White child, these children's underachievement is not defined as a learning disability. Instead, it is defined as a consequence of their inadequate socialization, in which case they may become identified as emotionally disturbed, or if they score low enough on an I.Q. test, as educable mentally retarded. The immediate consequence of their underidentification as learning disabled is that the children who do, in fact, need specific academic remediation, will be ignored and therefore not realize their potential.

When, as this study has illustrated, school officials define a child's noncompliant behavior as a symptom of illness, the responsibility for the behavior rests within the child. Rather than engaging in an ecological assessment of the child, which would explore the behavior of the child across settings and the responses of significant individuals to the child within those settings, most school systems engage only in psychological assessments, such as those seen in Lakeside, that focus on discovering the intellectual and/or emotional deficits that exist within the child. In so doing, the school is failing to recognize what actually is occurring between individuals, each of whom represents a system of beliefs as well as his or her unique abilities, which are manifested in his or her behavior.

Traditional methods of assessment yield results that validate the over and underrepresentation of different groups of children in different disability designations. Minority children and children from lower socioeconomic backgrounds, as a group, score lower on tests of intelligence and achievement than do middle-class White children. However, Mercer (1973) has demonstrated that these lower scores are not valid measures of the low-income child's potential, but rather demonstrate the degree to which the child has become assimilated into the dominant culture. In order to get an accurate assessment of a child's skills, psychologists will need to engage in ecologically oriented assessments that would place the child's functioning within the context of his or her experiences. In the case of understanding the behavior of children in schools, the culture of the community and the school system's place within it must also be understood. For an individual child, his or her behavior must be seen in the context of the school building he or she attends, as well as the culture of the classroom.

By following an ecological perspective in assessment, it certainly would be difficult to label any child as emotionally disturbed. Once behavior is understood in the context of its culture, it is difficult to perceive it as "insane." How can the schools then provide services to children who are obviously not able to function in the system as it now exists? Classification schemes have been developed as a means of facilitating communication between professionals as well as aiding in the bureaucratic functioning of a complex educational system. Hobbs' (1976) lengthy investigation of the issues surrounding the classification of children concluded that some sort of classification system is indeed necessary. It has also been recognized that, no matter what classification scheme is used, it would be impossible to completely avoid the cultural bias inherent in classifying individuals (Prugh, Engel & Morse, 1976).

In *The Futures of Children*, Hobbs suggests that we move away from the labeling of children as a means of identifying their needs. Instead, he calls for the development of a profile in which the child is no longer the sole focus of assessment and intervention. The role of the parents, the competencies of the child in his or her many environments, and the interventions to be used should be described. Interventions would be aimed at "points of discordance—discrepancy between the way that one individual in the system is behaving and the way that others who are important to him expect him to behave or wish he would behave"(p. 119).

Children who are experiencing problems relating to each other and to adults, and who are clearly troubled by the circumstances of their lives do exist. With the increasing number of single mothers and dependent children on welfare, and the decreasing employment opportunities and limited community supports available to these families, we can expect that there will be more troubled children in our urban schools in the coming years. Many of these children will be among those labeled as emotionally disturbed. Despite this, they will still be underserved. These children will not receive the education they need to break out of the cycle of poverty in which their mothers find themselves. They will not be exposed to models of behavior that will present an alternative way of solving problems. Their parents will not be offered the support they could use to help manage their children. Instead, these children will be punished, stigmatized, and segregated from the very kinds of experiences they need.

P.L. 94–142 was not intended as a funding and programming tool to be used by school districts for the segregation of difficult to manage children. It was developed to ensure that children who had, in the past, been excluded from a public education would have equal access to an education that would be appropriate to their needs and abilities. Thus a blind child would receive instruction in braille or through "talking books" at no additional cost to his or her family; a child with cerebral palsy would be provided with the adaptive equipment that would enable the child to see the chalkboard and hold a pencil; and an intellectually limited child would be provided instruction that would proceed at a pace that was commensurate with his or her rate of learning. These goals have been accomplished in many school districts throughout the United States.

Unfortunately, since this legislation rests on a deficit model of defining handicapping conditions it has not demanded any significant alterations in the American educational system that might have made it more responsive to the heterogeneous population it serves. This heterogeneity includes children who are physically and intellectually different from the average child, as well as those who have been raised in families whose cultural styles and beliefs vary from those of the "average American." Instead, special education is often delivered in segregated classrooms, where groups of deviant children are set off from their peers, only reinforcing their deviance in the eyes of others and, at the same time, reinforcing the stereotypical image of a normal, average child. Such a child is indeed imaginary. P.L. 94–142 has perhaps reinforced this image.

It is difficult to sort out how much of the change that we now see in the educational system's response to handicapped children is merely a surface compliance to the law, and how much represents a true commitment to the law's intent. One source of this problem is that the law was written from a perspective that focuses on children's problems in school and in society as coming from within the child rather than being an end product of his or her interactions with the demands and expectations of society, as reflected by the school system. This does not mean that some children do not have handicapping conditions that may place limits on their functional skills, but rather that schools stigmatize such children by the very classification systems and service-delivery models that have been developed, i.e., a special education system that permits the regular education system to continue, unaltered, by providing an escape valve for children who do not fit.

Bibliography

Aichorn, A. *Wayward Youth*. New York: Viking Press, 1935.

Algozzine, B. "The Disturbing Child: What You See is What You Get." *Alberta Journal of Abnormal Education Research* 22 (1976):330-33.

Algozzine, B. "The Emotionally Disturbed Child: Disturbed or Disturbing?" *Journal of Abnormal Child Psychology* 5 (1977):205-11.

Algozzine, B. & Curran, T.J. "Teacher's Predictions of Children's School Success as a Function of Their Behavior Tolerances." *Journal of Education Research* 72 (July-August, 1979):344-47.

Andersen, K. "A Threat to the Future." *Time*, May 14, 1984, p. 20.

Apter, S.J. *Troubled Children, Troubled Systems*. N.Y.: Pergammon Press, Inc., 1982.

Axline, V.M. "Play Therapy: Procedures and Results." In *Educating Emotionally Disturbed Children: Readings*, edited by H. Dupont, pp. 266-74. N.Y.: Holt, Rinehart & Winston, 1969.

Baratz, S.J. & Baratz, J.C. "Early Childhood Intervention: The Social Science Base of Institutional Racism." In *To See Ourselves: Anthropology and Modern Social Issues*. edited by T. Weaver. Glenview, Ill.: Scott Foresman & Co., 1973.

Becker, H.S. "Social Class Variations in Teacher-Pupil Relationships." *Journal of Educational Sociology* 25 (April 1952):451-65.

Becker, H.S. *Outsiders: Studies in the Sociology of Deviance*. Glenco, Ill: The Free Press, 1963.

Becker, H.S. *Sociological Work*. Chicago: Aldine Publishing, 1970.

Beers, C.W. *A Mind That Found Itself: An Autobiography*. New York: Longmans Green, 1908.

Berkowitz, P.H. & Rothman, E.P., eds. *Public Education for Disturbed Children in New York City*. Springfield, Ill: Charles C. Thomas, 1967.

Blumer, H. *Symbolic Interactionism*. Englewood Cliffs, N.J.: Prentice Hall, 1969.

Bogdan, R. & Kugelmass, J. "Case Studies of Mainstreaming: A Symbolic Interactionist Approach to Special Schooling." In *Special Education and Social Interests*, edited by L. Barton & S. Tomlinson. pp. 173-91. London: Croom Helm, 1984.

Bogdan, R. & Taylor, S. *Introduction to Qualitative Research Methods*. New York: John Wiley, 1975.

Bower, E.M. *Early Identification of Emotionally Handicapped Children In Schools*. Springfield, Ill: Charles C. Thomas, 1969.

Bronfenbrenner, U. "Reality and Research in the Ecology of Human Development." JSAS *Catalog of Selected Documents in Psychology* (Ms. No. 1333) 94, 1976.

Bronfenbrenner, U. "Toward an Experimental Ecology of Human Development." *American Psychologist* 32 (1977):513-31.

Buckholdt, D.R. & Gubrium, J.F. *Caretakers: Treating Emotionally Disturbed Children* Beverly Hills, Ca.: Sage Publications, Inc. 1979.

Budoff, M. "Providing Special Education Without Special Classes." *Journal of School Psychology* 10 (1972):199-205.

Chesler, P. *Women and Madness*. Garden City, N.Y.: Doubleday & Co., Inc. 1972.

Cone, J.D. & Hawkins, R.P. *Behavorial Assessment: New Directions in Clinical Psychology*. New York: Bruner/Mazel, Inc., 1977.

Conrad, P. & Schneider, C.V. *Deviance and Medicalization: From Badness to Sickness*. St. Louis, Missouri: C.V. Mosby Co., 1980.

Cross, W.E., Jr. "Black Families and Black Identity Development: Rediscovering the Distinction Between Self-esteem and Reference Group Orientation." International Seminar on the Child and the Family. (Mimeographed) St. Peter, Minn: Gustavus Adolphus College, 1979.

Crowe, W.E. & MacGinite, W.H. "The Influence of Student's Speech Characteristics on Teachers Evaluations of Oral Answers." *Journal of Educational Psychology* 66 (1974):304-08.

Curran, T.J. *The Influence of Ecological Fit on Teachers' Expectations*. Ph.D. Dissertation, Pennsylvania State University, 1977.

Des Jarlais, D.C. "Mental Illness as Social Deviance." In *A Study of Child Variance* (Vol. I), edited by W. Rhodes & M. Tracy, pp. 259-322, Ann Arbor: University of Michigan Press, 1977.

Distar Reading I. 2nd ed. Chicago: Science Research Associates, 1974.

Dunn, L. "Special Education for the Mildly Retarded: Is Much of It Justified?" *Exceptional Children* 35 (1968): 5-22.

Education for All Handicapped Children Act of 1975 (P.L. 94-142). In *Public Policy and the Education of Exceptional Children*, edited by F.J. Weintraub, A. Abeson, J. Ballard, and M. Lavor Reston, Va.: Council for Exceptional Children, 1976.

Engelmann, S. *Preventing Failure in the Primary Grades*. New York: Simon & Schuster, 1969.

Engelmann, S., Osborn, J., & Engelmann, T. *Distar Language: An Instructional System*. Chicago: Science Research Associates, 1969.

Erikson, E. *Childhood and Society*. New York: W.W. Norton & Co., Inc., 1963.

Finn, J.D. "Expectations and the Educational Environment." *Review of Education Research* 2 (1972):387-410.

Foster, G.G.; Ysseldyke, J.E.; & Reese, J.A. "I Wouldn't Have Seen It If I Hadn't Believed It." *Exceptional Children* 41 (1975):469-473.

Foster, S.L. & Richey, W.L. "Issues in the Assessment of Social Competence in Children." *Journal of Applied Behavorial Analysis* 12 (1979):625-638.

Gajar, A. "Educable Mentally Retarded, Learning Disabled, Emotionally Disturbed: Similarities and Differences." *Exceptional Children* 45 (1977):470-472.

Gillung, T.B. & Rucker, C.N. "Labels and Teacher Expectations." *Exceptional Children* 43 (1977):464-465.

Grier, W.H. & Cobbs, P.M. *Black Rage.* New York: Bantam Books, 1968.

Grosenick, J.K. & Huntze, S.L. *National Needs Analysis in Behavior Disorders: Severe Behavior Disorders.* Columbia, Missouri: Dept. of Special Education, University of Missouri, July 1980.

Guidubaldi, J. & Perry, J. "Divorce, Socioeconomic Status, and Children's Cognitive-Social Competence at School Entry." *American Journal of Orthopsychiatry* 54 (1984):459-68.

Hale, J. "Black Children: Their Roots, Culture, and Learning Styles". In *Understanding the Multicultural Experience in Early Childhood Education*, edited by O.N. Saracho & B. Spodek. Washington, D.C.: National Association for the Education of Young Children, 1983.

Hallahan, D.P. & Kauffman, J.M. "Labels, Categories, Behaviors: E.D., L.D., and E.M.R. reconsidered." *Journal of Special Education* 11 (1977):139-149.

Henry, J. *Culture Against Man.* New York: Random House, 1963.

Henry, J. "Education of the Negro child." In *Anthropological Perspectives on Education*, edited by M.L. Wax, S. Diamond, & F.O. Gearing. pp. 273-289. New York: Basic Books, 1971.

Hobbs, N. *The Futures of Children.* San Francisco: Jossey-Bass, 1975.

Hobbs, N., ed. *Issues in the Classification of Children* Vols. I & II. San Francisco: Jossey-Bass, 1976.

Hobbs, N. "An Ecologically Oriented, Service-Based System for the Classification of Handicapped Children," In *The Ecosystem of the "Sick" Child*, edited by S. Salzinger, J. Antrobus, & Glick. New York: Academic Press, 1980.

Hollingshead, A. & Redlich, F. *Social Class and Mental Illness: A Community Study.* New York: John Wiley & Sons, 1958.

Hurley, R. *Poverty and Mental Retardation: A Causal Relationship.* New York: Vintage Books, 1966.

Itard, J.M.G. *The Wild Boy of Averyon* Trans. by G.M. Humphrey New York: Appleton-Century Crofts, 1962. (Originally published in 1894.)

Jeffers, C. *Living Poor.* Ann Arbor, Mich: Ann Arbor Publishers, 1967.

Jones, R.L., ed. *Mainstreaming and the Minority Child.* Reston, Va.: Council for Exceptional Children, 1976.

Jones, R.L.; Gottlieb, J.; Guskin, S.; & Yoshida, R.K. "Evaluating Mainstreaming Programs: Models, Caveats, Considerations and Guidelines." *Exceptional Children* 44 (1798): 588-601.

Kardiner, A. "Explorations in Negro Personality." In *Culture and Mental Health*. edited by M.K. Opler. New York: Macmillan, 1959.

Katz, M. *Class, Bureaucracy, and Change: The Illusion of Educational Change in America*. New York: Praeger, 1971.

Kauffman, J. *Characteristcs of Children's Behavior Disorders* . 2nd ed. Columbus, Ohio: Charles E. Merrill Publishing Co., 1981.

Kitsuse, J. "Societal Reaction to Deviant Behavior: Problems of Theory and Method." In *The Other Side*, edited by H.M. Becker. New York: Free Press, 1964.

Knoblock, P. *Teaching Emotionally Disturbed Children*. Boston: Houghton Mifflin, 1983.

Laing, R.D. *The Politics of Experience and the Bird of Paradise*. New York: Penguin, 1967.

Leacock, E. *Teaching and Learning in City Schools*. New York: Basic Books, 1969.

Lindblad-Goldberg, M. & Dukes, J.L. "Support in Black, Low-Income, Single-Parent Families: Normative and Dysfunctional Patterns." *American Journal of Orthopsychiatry* 55 (1985):42-58.

Long, N.J.; Morse, W.C.; & Newman, R.D., eds. *Conflict in the Classroom: The Education of the Emotionally Disturbed Child*. 4th ed. Belmont, Ca.: Wadsworth Publishing Co., 1980.

Lora v. The Board of Education of the City of New York, et al. #75-C0917, U.S. District Court, E.D. N.Y., June 2, 1978.

Malcolm X. *The Autobiography of Malcolm X*. New York: Grove Press, 1966.

Malzberg, B. *New Data on Mental Disease Among Negroes in New York State*. Albany, N.Y.: Research Foundation for Mental Hygiene, 1965.

Mash, E.J. & Terdal, L.G. *Behavioral Assessment of Childhood Disorders*. New York: The Guildford Press, 1981.

Mead, M. *Coming of Age in Samoa*. New York: Mentor Books, 1949.

Mercer, J.R. *Labeling the Mentally Retarded: Clinical and Social System Perspectives on Mental Retardation*. Berkeley: University of California Press, 1973.

Merton, R.K. *Social Theory and Social Structure*. London: Free Press of Glencoe, 1957.

Miller, J.B. "Psychological Recovery in Low-Income, Single Parents." *American Journal of Orthopsychiatry* 52 (1982):346-52.

Moynihan, D.P. *The Negro Family: The Case for National Action*. Washington, D.C.: U.S. Dept. of Labor, 1965.

Nelson, C.C. & Schmidt, L.J. "The Question of the Efficacy of Special Classes." *Exceptional Children* 37 (1977):381-84.

Ogbu, J.U. *The Next Generation*. New York: Academic Press, 1974.

O'Leary, K.D. "The Assessment of Psychopathology in Children." In *Psychopathological Disorders of Childhood*, edited by H. Quay & J. Werry. John Wiley & Sons, 1972.

Parker, S. & Kleiner, R. *Mental Illness in the Urban Negro Community.* New York: Free Press, 1976.

Pidgeon, D.A. *Expectation and Pupil Performance.* Stockholm: Almquist & Wiksell, 1970.

Prugh, D.G.; Engel, M.; & Morse, W.C. "Emotional Disturbance in Children." In *Issues in the Classification of Children.* Vol. I, edited by N. Hobbs. San Francisco: Jossey-Bass, 1975.

Quay, H.C. & Galvin, J.P. *The Education of Behaviorially Disordered Children in the Public School Setting.* Interim report. Philadelphia, Pa.: Temple University, October 1970. (ERIC Document Reproduction Service no. ED 053 523.)

Rainwater, L. & Yancy, W.L. *The Moynihan Report and the Politics of Controversy.* Cambridge, Mass: M.I.T. Press, 1967.

Redl, F. & Wineman, D. *The Aggressive Child.* New York: The Free Press, 1957.

Reynolds, M.C. & Birch J.W. Teaching Exceptional Children in All American Schools. Reston, Va: Council for Exceptional Children, 1977.

Rhodes, W.C. "A Community Participation Analysis of Emotional Disturbance." *Exceptional Children* 36 (1970): 309-14.

Rhodes, W.C. *Behavorial Threat and Community Response.* New York: Behavorial Publications, Inc. 1972.

Rhodes, W.C. & Gibbins, S. "Community Programming for the Behavorially Deviant Child." In *Psychopathological Disorders of Childhood,* edited by H.C. Quay & J.S. Werry. New York: John Wiley & Sons, 1972.

Rhodes, W.C. & Tracy, M.L. *A Study of Child Variance,* Vols I & II. Ann Arbor: University of Michigan Press, 1972.

Riessman, F. *The Culturally Deprived Child.* Harper & Row, Publishers, 1962.

Rist, R. "Student Social Class and Teacher Expectations: The Self-Fulfilling Prophesy in Ghetto Education." *Harvard Educational Review* 40 (1970):411-450.

Rist, R. *The Urban School: A Factory for Failure.* Cambridge, Mass: M.I.T. Press, 1973.

Rist, R. *The Invisible Children: School Integration in American Society.* Cambridge, Mass: Harvard University Press, 1977.

Rist, R. & Harrell, J. "Labeling and the Learning Disabled Child: The Social Ecology of Educational Practice." *American Journal of Orthopsychiatry* 52 (1982):146-60.

Rosenhan, D.L. "On Being Sane in Insane Places." *Science,* January 1973, pp 250-58.

Rosenthal, R. & Jacobson, L. *Pygmalion in the Classroom.* New York: Holt, Rinehart & Winston, 1968.

Ross, A.O. *Psychological Disorders of Children,* 2nd ed. New York: McGraw Hill, 1980.

Ross, M.R. & Salvia, J.A. "Attractiveness as a Biasing Factor on Teacher Judgements." *American Journal of Mental Deficiency* 80 (1975):96-98.

Rubington, E. & Weinberg, M.S. *Deviance: The Interactionist Perspective.* 2nd ed. New York: Macmillan, 1973.

Rubovits, P.C. & Maehr, M.L. "Pygmalion Black and White." *Journal of Personality and Social Psychology* 25 (1973):210-18.

Ryan,W. *Blaming the Victim.* New York: Vintage Books, 1971.

Salvia, J. & Yesseldyke, J.E. *Assessment in Special and Remedial Education.* Boston: Houghton Mifflin, 1978.

Salvia, T.A. & Meisels, C.J. "Observer Bias: A Methodological Consideration in Special Education Research." *Journal of Special Education* 14 (1980):261-70.

Salzinger, S., Antrobus, J., & Glick, J. *The Ecosystem of the "Sick" Child.* New York: Academic Press, 1980.

Sarason, S.B. *The Culture of the School and the Problem of Change.* Boston: Allyn & Bacon, 1971.

Sarason, S.B. & Doris, J. *Educational Handicap, Public Policy and Social History.* New York: Free Press, 1979.

Scheff, T. *Being Mentally Ill: A Sociological Theory.* New York: Aldine Publishing Co., 1966.

Scheff, T. "The Labeling Theory of Mental Illness." *American Sociological Review* 39 (1974): 444-52.

Schlosser, L. & Algozzine, B. "The Disturbing Child: He or She?" *Alberta Journal of Education Research* 25 (1979): 30-36.

Silverstein, B. & Krate, R. *Children of the Dark Ghetto: A Developmental Psychology.* New York: Praeger Publishers, 1975.

Strole, L. & Fischer, A.K., eds. *Mental Health in the Metropolis—The Mid-Town Manhattan Study.* New York: N.Y.U. Press, 1971.

Swap, S. "Disturbing Classroom Behaviors: A Developmental and Ecological View. *Exceptional Children* 41 (1974): 162-71.

Swap, S. "The Ecological Model of Emotional Disturbance in Children: A Status Report and Proposed Synthesis." *Behavorial Disorders* 3 (1978):186-96.

Szasz, T. *The Myth of Mental Illness.* New York: Harper & Row, 1966.

Szasz, T. *The Age of Madness.* New York: Jason Aronson, 1974.

U.S. Bureau of the Census. "Metropolitan Area Definition and a Re-evaluation of Concept and Statistical Practice. Working paper No. 28. Washington, D.C., 1969.

U.S. Department of Commerce. *1980 Census of Population and Housing.* Washington, D.C.: Bureau of the Census, 1980.

U.S. Department of Commerce. *Supplementary Report: Provisional Estimates of Social, Economic and Housing Characteristics.* Washington, D.C.: Bureau of the Census, 1982.

U.S. General Accounting Office. *Disparities Still Exist in Who Gets Special Education.* Comptroller general's report to the chairman, Subcommittee on Select Education, Committee on Education and Labors, Washington, D.C.: House of Representative 1981.

Vacc, N.A. "Long Term Effects of Special Class Intervention for Emotionally Disturbed Children." *Exceptional Children* 39 (1972):15-22.

Vacc, N.A. & Keist, N. "Emotionally Disturbed Children and Regular Classroom Teachers." *Elementary School Journal* 77 (1977):309-17.

Valentine, C.A. *Culture and Poverty: Critique and Counter-Proposals.* Chicago: University of Chicago Press, 1968.

Wax, M.L. & Wax, R.H. "Great Tradition Little Tradition, and Formal Education." In *Anthropological Perspectives on Education*, edited by M.L. Wax, S. Diamond, & F.O. Gearing New York: Basic Books, 1971.

Wayson, W. "ESEA: Decennial Views of the Revolution, II The Negative side." *Phi Beta Kappan*, November 1975.

Werry, J.S. & Quay, H.C. "The Prevalence of Behavior Symptoms in Younger Elementary School Children. *American Journal of Orthopsychiatry* 41 (1971):136-143.

Willie, C.V. *The Family Life of Black People.* Columbus, Ohio: Charles E. Merrill, 1970.

Wilson, S. "The Use of Ethnographic Techniques in Educational Research." *Review of Educational Research* 47 (1977):245-65.

Wortman, R.A. "Depression, Danger, Denial: Working with Poor, Black, Single Parents." *American Journal of Orthopsychiatry* 51 (1981):662-71.

Ysseldyke, J. & Foster, G. "Bias in Teachers' Observations of Emotionally Disturbed-Learning Disabled Children." *Exceptional Children* 44 (1978):613-15.

Index